Be Supernatural

Activation Manual

Kim and Shari Babcock

Dedication

We dedicate this book to:

• Lynn and Christine Thompson, Shari's parents, whose hunger for the Lord and intense search to know Him better ignited the same desires in the hearts of their two daughters.

• Margaret Babcock, Kim's mom, who modeled how to forgive and act like Jesus.

• To our children, Jeremiah & Bethany, Becky, Jonathan & Valerie, Lucas & Rachel, who are also living the adventure.

• And to our grandchildren: Ethan, Elyssa, Levi, Noah and those to come—who will live their entire lives surrounded by the knowledge that God is a good Father, that Jesus died so that they could be in God's family and that the Holy Spirit is willing to share His power with them so that they can have adventures with Him every single day.

ACKNOWLEDGEMENTS

Thank you to our daughter, Becky, for sharing what she learned during her time working for Bethel church and attending BSSM (Bethel School of Supernatural Ministry). Thank you for returning to Argentina to direct the School of Extreme Formation (EFX) and begin the School of the Supernatural (ESN) in Catedral de la Fe. And thank you for your writing contributions in a few of these chapters.

Thank you, Karen Ferreyra, Lucas Marin, Malena Godoy, Carolina Barraza, Fernanda Thomas, Cecilia Puchulutegui & Natalia Arraigada for showing infinite patience in helping me with the grammar in the Spanish edition. May the Lord multiply the number of diamonds in your crowns!

Thank you to Margaret Wrasse, an amazing English professor and awesome friend who dedicated hours and hours to helping us get an edited English copy into the hands of our readers. Also, thank you, Mary Sprague, for buying and proofreading the first copy. You're a soul sister.

Thank you to the Castle kids (Castilleros) and leaders of Argentina. Your passion for the Lord has converted into hundreds of testimonies of salvations, healings, deliverances and miracles. What adventures we have had in the past, present and will continue to have in the future with our incredible God. Let's continue to cross the chicken line!

Thank you to our national King's Castle (CDR) staff/team -- those serving with us presently and those who have served in the past. Without you, the ministry of CDR Argentina would not exist.

Thank you to the students of the School of Extreme Formation, EFX, of 2017 and 2018. You have contributed many of the stories and testimonies used in this book. We thank God for the passion that lives in each one of you to serve and take risks for the Lord.

Thank you to Emmanuel Susbiela, our extraordinary Spanish editor who always encourages, advises, corrects and basically does everything to help us get our Spanish edition printed. He also tweaked the cover and designed the back of the English edition. Thank you so much for all your work!

Thank you to Fabio Lelli who originally designed the cover in English and Spanish. Also to Josh Canjura who upgraded the treasure map.

ENDORSEMENTS

It is my joy to endorse Kim and Shari Babcock and their new book, *Be Supernatural*! By God's grace I served over twenty-five years in both district and national leadership in the Assemblies of God. It was rare for me to find a supernatural and prophetic couple like Kim and Shari who understood the power of releasing genuinely prophetic words over people's destinies. Many churches with which I was acquainted actually believed in supernatural spiritual gifts, but did very little to help their members activate these gifts. That's what I love about this book. Not only is it full of Scriptures, teaching, and testimonies, it includes many practical activation exercises any believer may use to sharpen their walk in the realm of the supernatural. Reading this book will help you develop ears that hear and eyes that see. Get ready for dreams, visions, and encounters in the unseen realm with the Holy Spirit.

Rev. Dave Williams
Dave Williams Ministries
Author: *Hope in the Last Days, Skill for Battle,*
The Art of Pacesetting Leadership

This book is a living testimony to what God can do through Holy Spirit filled teenagers. You will be captured, intrigued and surprised as you read what happens when youth are inspired and equipped to reach out with the love of Jesus Christ... in the power of Holy Spirit.

Upon receiving the manuscript of this book, my wife, Janie and I sat together and read several chapters. We both got excited about its potential, not just for youth. Adults, Bible class teachers, small-group leaders, pastors and evangelists of all ages will be inspired and thrust into action.

The format of these brief chapters is simple: a title, a proposition, then powerful testimonies that display the truth of that proposition in practice. It is an easy, exciting read... an excellent tool.

I have witnessed Kim and Shari Babcock's joyful, effective leadership with the King's Castle youth in Argentina. They live, teach and breathe in the supernatural. Watch out! It is contagious!

Ralph Hiatt
Author: *Argentina a Love Story*
Missionary to Argentina for more than 40 years

I would like to recommend this book, not only for the scriptures and deep teachings that you will find within but also for what is behind the book, the lives of Kim and Shari Babcock. They are two people with an incredible love for what they do, who know a supernatural God and whose hearts' desire is to pour their life and experience into these pages.

I want to encourage you to read this book because it will awaken something in your spirit and you will have the opportunity to know a God of miracles; a real God, a close God, a God who is present every moment. You will not only receive an intellectual impartation, but every chapter will give you a chance to personally activate, or put into practice, what you have just learned. I recommend that you read this book and open your heart to experience a supernatural God.

Osvaldo Carnival
Pastor of Cathedral of Faith, Buenos Aires
Author and Church planter

Kim and Shari Babcock are true followers of Jesus who genuinely desire others to experience His Presence and power. They have given their lives to train others to be sensitive to the leading of the Holy Spirit and to learn to act on those leadings. This book comes out of real-life experience and will be a help to all those with a similar desire to expand the Kingdom of God.

Rev. Jeff Hlavin
Michigan District Supt. of the Assemblies of God

TABLE OF CONTENTS

INTRODUCTION

Whoever claims to live in him must live as Jesus did.
1 John 2:6

In no way will this manual satisfy all doctrinal issues. That is the job of each individual, to study to show himself approved. (2 Tim. 2:15) The purpose of this book is to push readers out of their comfort zones and win the lost to Jesus through deeper intimacy with God, personal spiritual growth and power encounters.

The Bible clearly states in 1 John "*as He is, so are we in this world*" and "*we ought to live as Jesus did.*" Jesus couldn't even leave the house without something supernatural happening. He affected the eternity of everyone He met, tore down damaging cultural taboos and ruined every funeral He ever attended. There was so much life flowing out from Him that sickness and death had to flee from His Presence. And we get to "*live as Jesus did*" according to the apostle John!

Acts 2:17-18 tells us that in these last days, EVERY HUMAN is a candidate to receive an outpouring of the Holy Spirit in their lives, **no matter the age, gender or economic status.** This Holy Spirit deluge is coming whether it fits into our theology or not. So let's get ready to equip and receive a generation full of the Spirit, walking in

His power and developing the gifts in order to bring in the greatest harvest that the world has ever seen!

Many of the testimonies in this activation manual have come out of the ministry of *King's Castle Argentina* (CDR), the *School of Extreme Formation* (EFX)—both under the jurisdiction of the Argentine Assemblies of God—and the *Supernatural School* (ESN) of Catedral de la Fe, which is an influential church in Buenos Aires. Since we, along with our daughter, Becky, work with these ministries, we have first-hand knowledge and access to their testimonies.

Our family has also been heavily influenced by some of the teachings and the evangelistic methods of Bethel Church in Redding CA and their school, BSSM. When our daughter, Becky, attended the school, she would call us and tell us the innovative ways to evangelize that she was learning in BSSM. We would call our staff together, explain it to them and begin to practice the same. Then we would begin to teach the Castle kids, or Castilleros, around the country that particular method, and as the Holy Spirit impacted lives, the testimonies would flow in. In the past, we've jokingly referred to CDR Argentina as Bethel's southern laboratory that they didn't even know existed.

As stated above, this book is by no means complete but it is our starting point and will hopefully spur the reader on to take risks for God, see people come to know Jesus, and give you many testimonies of your own. May God continue to equip us with His mighty Holy Spirit, His gifts and the courage to take risks on His behalf. And may we remember that Love must be the basis for everything we do.

Kim & Shari Babcock
AG Missionaries
Buenos Aires, Argentina

ACTIVATION #1 — HEARING GOD

My sheep listen to my voice; I know them, and
they follow me. John 10:27

Call to me and I will answer you and tell you
great and unsearchable things you
do not know. Jeremiah 33:3

It is normal for family members to talk to one another, but we also need to listen. In the same way, God wants to talk to us because we are his sons and daughters. God speaks in many different ways, but however He speaks it will always line up with His Word, the Bible. Some of the ways that He speaks to us include:

- The Bible (when we read it, His Spirit "translates" it for us, or shows us how to apply it to our lives.
- Audible voice (Samuel heard God 3 times,1 Sam. 3; Saul on the Damascus road, Acts 9)
- Audible voice inside (It is so loud inside of us that we think others can hear it)
- Still small voice (comes like a thought, or a series of thoughts, 1 Kings 19:12)
- Mental picture (when using your spiritual eyes, Ephesians 1:18)
- Conviction of sin (John 16:8)

- He will show you things to come (John 16:13)
- Angelic visitation (Daniel)
- Open visions (Peter and the sheet that came down from heaven)

Testimonies

A seven-year-old approached her leader after the group spent time hearing God, and said, "God told me that I can't steal things any more."

Another girl from the neighborhood, during an activation on hearing God, felt like God told her that He wanted to give her "His love and His heart".

A twelve-year-old shut his eyes and immediately saw the words, "I will always be with you!

Vanina, (18 years old) was frustrated because while her team members of King's Castle ministry were hearing God's voice, she wasn't. So the next week, she decided to pass every spare moment of her free time between classes at the Bible school in the prayer chapel asking God to speak to her. Finally, on Thursday night, she heard God's whisper, "You are going to meet a girl this weekend during the training, and she has been raped by an uncle."

Vani wasn't looking for that kind of information and didn't know what to do.

"How will I know who it is?" she asked God.

"I'll show you," came the answer.

The next night, Vani traveled to King's Castle Headquarters

to help lead a training weekend for forty teenagers. During the ministry time, everyone responded to the invitation to deepen their walk with God—with the exception of one girl, who seemed very unplugged. She hadn't participated in any of the activities and sat with a bored attitude.

"That is the girl," she sensed God say.

Vani approached the teenager. "Hi," she said.

The girl turned the other way, ignoring her.

Finally Vani said, "I know that you have been molested."

The girl's head swiveled around and she looked at Vani in horror. "Who told you?"

"God did," Vani responded, "because He knows that the only way that you are going to get healed is by repenting of your own sins and letting Him heal you. Do you want to receive Jesus as your Savior and Healer?

The girl began to cry. "Yes, I do!"

Vani hugged her and introduced her to Jesus. That night the young lady received Jesus as Savior and healer and was set free from a spirit of fear.

David, (age 10) along with his siblings and cousins, **was encouraged to listen to God** during family devotions. Quiet worship music played in the background and everyone waited quietly for the Lord to speak to them. After a little while, everyone began to share what they heard, saw, or felt. David's aunt looked at him directly and asked, "What did God show you?"

Without missing a beat, he answered, "I saw Jesus in a river with a bunch of people. He saw me on the bank and invited me in to play. So I jumped in, too."

Since then, David has maintained his relationship with Jesus, never getting out of the river. He has made many godly choices in his life. Today he is married to a wonderful Christian and they are committed to walking daily with God.

Activation: Get comfortable with your Bible and a notebook. (Put your cell phone on silent.)

1. Spend time thanking God for being good.

2. Ask Him to cleanse you from every sin, mistake and doubt in the name of Jesus. Surrender to him every worry, fear and frustration. If you think He doesn't want to talk to you, repeat: "I rebuke the lie that God doesn't want to talk to me, in Jesus' name."

3. Tell God that you want to hear whatever He has to say. Expect Him to communicate with you. You can ask Him specific questions like, "Jesus, what do you like about me?"

4. Write or draw what you hear, see or feel.

Optional Activation:

1. Ask God, "How do you see me? What do you want me to know about You? (Or another question, or wait for Him to start the conversation.)

2. Write or draw what you hear, see or feel.

*Note: If there is a day when you do not hear anything, you still win because Isaiah 64:4 tells us the He acts on behalf of the one who waits on Him.

ACTIVATION #2
THE POWER OF GOD'S WORD

For the word of God is alive and active. Sharper than any double-edged sword, it penetrates even to dividing soul and spirit, joints and marrow; it judges the thoughts and attitudes of the heart. Hebrews 4:12

All Scripture is God-breathed and is useful for teaching, rebuking, correcting and training in righteousness, so that the servant of God may be thoroughly equipped for every good work. 2 Tim. 3:16-17

And pray in the Spirit on all occasions with all kinds of prayers and requests. With this in mind, be alert and always keep on praying for all the Lord's people. Ephesians 6:17

The Bible is infallible, powerful and eternal. When we read and study the Bible, we learn how to think and talk like God. No matter what problem we face there is a solution or a principle that will bring us to the solution. Therefore, if I have a financial problem, and pay tithes, I can remind God of Malachi 3:10, where He promises that if we tithe, God will open the windows of heaven and pour out upon us blessings that we cannot contain. If we are fearful, we can meditate on Luke 10:19 or Isa. 41:10 until the Word changes the way we think. If we believe that we can't do something, we can meditate on Phil. 4:13 until we understand that *we can do ALL things through Christ who gives us strength.*

Testimonies

*Sara, (20 years old) had a terrible cold but couldn't miss her microbiology class. Arriving at class, sneezing repeatedly with her nose running like a faucet, she was frustrated because she knew that God's plan was to heal since the Bible declared that 'by his wounds, we are healed' (Isa. 53:5). Sara found her seat, feeling terrible, when a verse popped into her head that she had memorized years before, ...*pray one for another, that you might be healed.* (James 5:16)

Suddenly, an idea came to her mind. *Every time I sneeze, I'm going to pray for someone.* Never had she linked praying for others to receiving her own healing.

Sara sneezed and prayed for the salvation of a schoolmate. Sneezed again and prayed for her professor to come to know Jesus as his Lord. Every time she sneezed or blew her nose, she prayed for someone. After a short time, she stopped sneezing so much, and her nose began to dry up. By the end of the class, all cold symptoms had disappeared!

*name changed

Rachel (16-years-old) entered the kitchen where her parents were having breakfast.

"I need a verse," she said, "that I can use to take down a shooter at the school, should it ever happen."

Her parents looked at her.

"1 John 4:4, Greater is He that is in you than the devil that's in the world," offered her mother.

"No weapon formed against you shall prosper...this is the heritage of the servants of the Lord..." said her dad.

"Don't forget to use the name of Jesus," her mom reminded her. "And you can use these verses from behind a desk."

"No, Mom. I have to rebuke them in the name of Jesus by the authority of these verses," Rachel answered. "Besides, if I die, I'm ready to go to heaven but I doubt that hardly any of my classmates would go to heaven if they died today."

She left for school and her parents spent more time than usual praying for her and for the security of the school that day.

When Kim was nine years old, the doctor found a cyst in one of his eyes and told him that he would need to have it removed surgically. Seeing that Kim was afraid of having surgery, his grandmother told him that God could heal him because the Bible declared that *by the wounds of Jesus, we are healed.* Kim began to pray and quoted the verse over and over concerning the cyst in his eye. The more he said the verse, the more he believed it and the more his faith grew. In the weeks following, the cyst began to grow smaller. Upon returning to the doctor, he was told that the cyst had disappeared. God is faithful to complete His Word.

Bella, Alejo and Dylan were sharing Jesus in Brazil with Castle kids from other countries. In two days they had witnessed eight miracles of healing and had seen many people give their lives to Jesus. One of the girls on their team, Alicia, suddenly felt a stab of pain in her back. When they asked those around them if anyone had back pain, a boy came forward to receive prayer. When the kids prayed for him, all the pain left and Alicia's did too!

Activation:

1. Think of a problem with which you need help.

2. Pick one of these themes and read the verses that go with it.

Salvation	2 Peter 3:9, Acts 16:33-34 (for your family)
Worry:	Phil. 4:6-7, 1 Peter 5:7
Self Control:	Titus 2:11-12, Prov. 25:28
Sickness:	Isa. 53:5, Exodus 15:26b 1 Peter 2:24
Fear:	Luke 19:10, Isaiah 41:10
Provision:	Phil. 4:19, Mal. 3:10
Forgiveness:	Matt. 6:14-15, Eph. 4:26-27
Protection:	1 John 4:4, Isa. 54:17, Ps. 34:7, Luke 10:19

3. These verses give the solution to the problem that you are facing. Declare them today, tomorrow and every day until these truths become part of your mindset. Write down the changes that happen in your life as you declare God's Word over your life.

4. Memorize these verses so you always have "the sword of the Spirit" ready for any and every situation.

ACTIVATION #3
KNOWING FATHER GOD

Jesus said to him, "I am the way, the truth and the life. No one comes to the Father except through Me.   John 14:6

Jesus answered and said to him, "If anyone loves Me, he will keep My word; and My Father will love him, and We will come to him and make Our home with him. John 14:23

We love Him because He first loved us. 1 John 4:19

After receiving Christ as Savior and starting to walk with the Lord, we can become very comfortable in our relationship with Jesus. We can approach Him, speak to Him, worship Him and feel peace in His presence. Nevertheless, many people have a complicated relationship with their earthly fathers that may affect how they see Father God. If you have been abandoned by your biological father, you may feel that Father God has no interest in your life either. If you were mistreated by your own dad, it may be easy to think that your heavenly Dad is also easily angered, rough, or so strict that you are not able to enjoy having a relationship with Him.

Testimonies

Melina, from Cordoba, is a15-year-old who attended a Summit where she was taught to hear the voice of God. After the teaching, everyone took time to listen to Him individually. (Each teenager had received a sheet of paper with questions that they were to ask God.) Melina, who was abandoned by her own father when very small, never felt very comfortable approaching God the Father. Nevertheless, she made the decision to be brave and asked the question, "Jesus, would you present me to Father God?"

Afterwards she followed up with the next question. "Father God, what do you think about me?

She closed her eyes and immediately saw something beautiful. In her own words she shares:

> *"Father God showed me a white candle and told me that it represented purity, transparency, delicacy and attention. Its long length and volume represented His love for me and all of it represented perfection. Then, I heard from the Holy Spirit that he loved me so much that every day he waits for me to come spend time with Him. He is an available God."*

Ayelén from the province of Buenos Aires shares:

"In one of our classes of EFX, I asked Jesus if He would present me to Father God. In that moment I saw a room full of light, it appeared as if I had just walked into heaven! Upon entering, I saw enormous hands that were moving as if they were rocking a baby. I sensed that I was that baby and that

Father God was showing me that I continue being his little girl. It was such a clear revelation of Him as my heavenly Dad."

Activation: Get comfortable, in a place where you can be free from interruptions. (Turn off the phone.)

Ask God the following questions:

1. What do you want to tell me, Jesus? (Write down His answer.)

2. Jesus, would you present me to your Father? (Write down what happens.)

3. Father God, what do you think of me? (Draw or describe what He shows you.

4. Holy Spirit, what do you want to show me? (Draw or describe what you see, hear or feel?)

Activation #4 — Identity

I will be a Father to you, and you will be my sons and daughters, says the Lord Almighty. 2 Cor. 6:18

For those who are led by the Spirit of God are the children of God. The Spirit you received does not make you slaves, so that you live in fear again; rather, the Spirit you received brought about your adoption to sonship.

And by Him we cry, "Abba, Father." The Spirit himself testifies with our spirit that we are God's children.
Romans 8:14-16

When we come to know Jesus as Savior, we are immediately accepted into His family. His Dad becomes our Dad and He freely gives us His Holy Spirit. But until we fully understand what it means to be sons and daughters of God, we may believe the lies that the enemy tells us to keep us from enjoying our family benefits. If satan can replace the truths of God, such as *God is good, He loves us, we are important to Him,* and *we can live like Jesus did,* he can rob us of our inheritance.

Jesus Christ died so that we could have a personal relationship with Father God. It is Father's desire that His family be united, sons and daughters with whom He can share His love, power, wisdom and more. The only power that satan has over us is if he can deceive us into believing a lie. If we can discern the truth in each situation, we can overcome sin, the devil, and the kingdom of darkness every time.

Testimony

Gastón, (age 18, from Misiones) **spent many years believing lies,** that although he was unaware of it, were destroying his identity and not allowing him to see God as He really is.

One day, in an EFX class (School of Extreme Formation), Gastón was challenged to examine his heart, under the guidance of the Holy Spirit and find the lies that he was believing about himself. The leader, Rich, a Bible professor from Bethel School of the Supernatural, knowing by a word of knowledge that Gastón needed to be free of lies, asked Gaston to stand up and declare the lies that he was believing about himself in order to bring them to the light. Trembling, but confident that Rich was not going to hurt him, Gastón stood up but couldn't speak until Rich approached him, put his hand on Gastón's shoulder, and began to pray over him in English. Seeing Rich's smile, (although not understanding a word) Gastón felt support both from Rich and from God and was able to speak out three lies that had become his reality.

"I'm a failure. I'm alone. I'm ugly." He couldn't hold back the tears and began to sob. There were no words to express the pain in his heart that he had carried for years, beginning when he father had abandoned him as a baby and through the years of abuse that had followed.

But Rich said, "Now, speak the opposite words. The truths of God. But before you do, we are all going to laugh at these lies that Gastón has been believing. We are going to mock satan's lies."

At first, Gastón didn't understand what was happening. He was crying but when everyone started to laugh at the lies, something began to shift on the inside of him. Rich hugged him and assured Gastón that **he was a beloved son of God.** A wave of love and hope washed over him and he began to declare the truths of God over himself.

"I'm able! I'm not alone! I'm good looking!"

"Repeat it again, louder this time," Rich instructed. And each time that Gastón repeated the truth, he received more inner healing and the presence of God increased until everyone in the room was affected. When he was finished, all his classmates took turns giving him a hug and Gastón has never been the same since.

Today, he is part of the national staff of CDR and has friends all over Argentina.

Activation:

1. Ask Jesus to show you if you are believing a lie about yourself.

2. Ask Jesus to show you where you first believed the lie.

3. Ask Jesus to show you where He was at the moment.

4. Ask Jesus to show you the truth.

5. Forgive whoever may have taught you the lie or caused you pain in this memory. Say to God, "I forgive_____ for_____.

6. Say to God, "I renounce the lie of _____ in the name of Jesus." Begin to declare the truth. Declare it until you are convinced. Ask Jesus to help you live and walk in that truth.[1]

Jesus is the truth and the Bible is full of truthful principles. The truth is always lined up with the Word of God.

Notes and Book Suggestions

[1]De Silva, Dawna and Teresa Liebscher. *Sozo, Saved, Healed, Delivered: A Journey into Freedom with the Father, Son, and Holy Spirit.* Shippensburg, PA: Destiny Image, 2016. p. 56.

ACTIVATION #5 — RECEIVING THE BAPTISM IN THE HOLY SPIRIT

Do not leave Jerusalem, but wait for the gift my Father promised, which you have heard Me speak about. For John baptized with water, but in a few days you will be baptized with the Holy Spirit. Acts 1:4-5

But you will receive power when the Holy Spirit comes on you; and you will be my witnesses in Jerusalem, and in all Judea and Samaria, and to the ends of the earth. Acts 1:8

If you then, though you are evil, know how to give good gifts to your children, how much more will your Father in heaven give the Holy Spirit to those who ask Him. Luke 11:13

The last words of Jesus before leaving to go to heaven were, "Wait for the promise of the Father because He will give you power to be my disciples, starting from where you live all the way to the ends of the earth." And Father God gave it to them in Acts Chapter 2. Peter, in the middle of his message, declared that the promise of the Father is for everyone and their children. (Acts 2:29) The baptism of the Holy Spirit, that comes with the evidence of speaking in unknown languages—a secret code between you and Father God that Satan cannot interrupt—is the inheritance of all the children of God. You can go to heaven without speaking in tongues, but why? If Father God wants to give you a gift of intimacy and power that will help you live a supernatural life, why wouldn't you want it?

Kim loves power tools, the more powerful the better. He can build furniture or a house with a hammer and saw, but he would much prefer to make it with an electric saw and a nail gun. Speaking in tongues is a spiritual power tool. When one prays in tongues, he is "plugging" his spirit into the throne of God and the current (Holy Spirit) of God fills him up. Speaking in tongues is a tool of prayer, intercession (Rom. 8:26-27) praise and worship (1 Cor. 14:14-15) edification, (Jude 1:20,1 Cor. 14:2) and power.

Satan doesn't want you receiving the baptism of the Holy Spirit with the accompanying prayer language because he can't interrupt this type of prayer, nor argue about what you are saying because you are praying from your spirit, not from your understanding. (1 Cor. 14:14-15) He knows that you are going to ruin his plans if you begin to pray in tongues every day; therefore, he has convinced many people that this promise isn't for everyone.

Don't let him rob you of something so beautiful and necessary. This is not the "gift of tongues" that 1 Cor. 14 verses 5 and 13 talk about that is used to edify the church when paired with the gift of interpretation. The baptism of the Holy Spirit in Acts 2, 10, and 19 is the *Promise* of Father God for EVERYONE and opens the door to all of the gifts. This will help you to *live as*

Jesus lived!

Testimonies

Milagros (age 15) from San Juan province, recently received the baptism of the Holy Spirit. She tells her story:

"I always wanted the baptism of the Holy Spirit with the blessing of speaking in tongues but I was believing the lie that it was for the adults and not for me. But when I understood that this gift from Father God was for everyone including me, I opened my mouth, and He filled it with His Spirit. I began to speak in other languages. I was so happy!

My mom has a tendency to faint. So far the doctors can't figure out why. When she does, she bangs her head and other parts of her body because no one knows when she is suddenly going to fall. A few days after I received the Holy Spirit, she fell down and stopped breathing. My dad ran to get the smelling salts to revive her and the Holy Spirit said to me, 'Pray in tongues.' During these episodes, my mom is completely limp, too heavy to lift, so I hugged just her head and shoulders to my heart and prayed over her fervently in tongues.

She woke up and began to breathe. Instead of being confused and disoriented as in other times, she began to cry and said, 'Mili! I felt a strong hug that woke me up, but my knee hurts so badly!'

Mili looked at her mom's knee and saw a big bump swelling over the kneecap. Guided again by the Holy Spirit, she commanded the swelling to go down and healing to come. Immediately, to her surprise, the swelling went down under her hand! Milagros fell in love with the Holy Spirit all over again that day and is so thankful for His presence in her daily life.

Aixa was one of two teens that left without having received the baptism of the Holy Spirit after a weekend CDR camp. All of the leaders, however, encouraged her to keep seeking God for it. A few days later, in Citizenship class at her high school, the teacher gave everyone a free period. So Aixa put in her ear buds in order to hear worship music and started singing softly to herself—and suddenly realized that she was singing in tongues!

Fourteen-year-old Ezequiel had a terror of speaking in public to the point that he had to give oral exams to his teachers in the hallway because he would faint if he stood in front of the class. But during a weekend CDR training, Ezequiel received the baptism in the Holy Spirit and his prayer language began to flow out of him. (John 7:37-39)

The following morning, the second day of training, he pulled Matías, a national team member, off to the side to tell him, "A miracle occurred last night on the way home! My team and I boarded a bus, and then I got up and preached to the people! And it was so awesome that when we changed buses, I did it again!"

Activation:

1. Ask God to forgive you and cleanse you from whatever He doesn't want in your life. Forgive those that need to be forgiven. Forgiveness isn't a feeling, but a decision that sets you free.

2. Ask Jesus to baptize you in the Holy Spirit, knowing that

God wants to do so. (Luke 11:13)

3. Receive it by faith. Begin to speak by faith. If you hear a syllable, say it. **You cannot fail.** We receive salvation by faith and we can receive the baptism in the Holy Spirit the same way.

4. Use what you get. If it is a sound, say it. If it is a phrase, speak it out. John 7:39 promises us that from our interior (belly) will flow rivers of living water, which is talking about the Spirit of God. Don't analyze it. It doesn't make sense to your natural mind because it's supernatural.

Note: The first thing that the enemy will tell you is that you are making it up. Don't listen to him. Believe that God is giving you what He has promised in Acts chapter 1 and 2:39.

5. Enjoy spending time with Him. Now you have a secret code between you and God; a language that satan will not be able to interrupt, tools of prayer, intercession, praise and worship. Expect the power of God to live big within you, to help you overcome sin and live in the supernatural.

Note: There is no shame in not having the baptism of the Holy Spirit if you are seeking Him. If you seek Him, you will find Him. This infilling is for whoever will run after Him shamelessly, clamoring for more of His Spirit and presence. Don't give up, this Promise is for you!

Activation #6 — Healing: Jesus Paid the Price

He was pierced for our transgression, He was crushed for our iniquities; the punishment that brought us peace was on Him and by His wounds we are healed. Isa. 53:5

When evening came, many who were demon-possessed were brought to Him, and He drove out the spirits with a word and healed all the sick. This was to fulfill what was spoken through the prophet Isaiah: "He took up our infirmities and bore our diseases." Matt. 8:16-17

He himself bore our sins in His body on the cross, so that we might die to sins and live for righteousness; "by His wounds you have been healed." 1 Peter 2:24

The most powerful and loving act in history was when Jesus died on the cross for us. We know that He paid the price so that we could be reconciled with Father God. Just that would have been sufficient, but God has an extravagant love for us. Jesus didn't only die for our sins, but also because of the wounds He suffered we can be healed!

When you pay your light bill, you are given a receipt that serves as a declaration that you indeed paid the bill. If someone tells you to pay it again, what will you do? Will you pay it again or show them your receipt? Obviously you will show them the receipt so that you don't have to pay it twice.

Jesus paid the price for our healing therefore we can always pray with confidence, knowing that God wants to heal the sick. When you pray for someone and they don't get healed, don't be discouraged but continue praying for others just the same. Jesus paid a very high price for our healing. This is why it is necessary that we fight for victory in this area. We want Jesus to get what He paid for with his suffering!

Testimonies

Some Castle teens went to a public pool to hang out together and saw a little girl with ugly scars on her leg. When they asked her what happened she told them that since she was very little she had many problems with the bones in her leg and foot. Then they saw that her foot was malformed, with the toes twisted one above another. As the kids began to pray, the bones of the toes began to move and went back into place! The little girl cried with joy to see her foot completely healed, every toe in the right spot!

Toti, (age 17) tells us what happened at a youth camp,

"I had scoliosis so bad that I was actually hunched over, and also had a small tumor attached to the deformed vertebras. When I was prayed for, I felt snapping and crackling in my back and I was able to stretch to my full height, and the tumor was gone!"

Malena (age 17, Buenos Aires) tells us:

"I saw a lady up ahead of me and felt like God told me that she had a broken heart and suffered depression. So I approached her and asked her if she was heartbroken about something.

'Yes!' she exclaimed. 'Yes, for a long time, and I am taking medication for depression.' We were able to pray with her, recommend a caring church, hug her and show that Jesus really loved her."

Activation:

1. Find someone who is sick. Before praying for this person, remember that Jesus already paid the price. He poured out His life so that this person could be healed!

2. If the person is suffering pain, ask him/her on a scale of one to ten how he/she feels. (1 being little pain and 10 being extreme pain.) This helps you be able to be able to see the change easily.

3. Pray a short, simple prayer. Then ask the person to move around, or see if he/she can do something that couldn't be done before. Ask if there is a change or not. If the pain left, thank the Lord. If the pain went down, rejoice in the change, and ask the person if you can pray one more time.

4. Pray again, short and simple. Have the person check it out again. Whatever the result, remind the person that he/

she is loved by God and that He wants to be a part of the person's daily life.

5. Ask the person if he/she knows this God that healed the sickness, or if they want to know Him.

Explain how to receive Jesus as Lord. Encourage the person to find a church where he/she can grow spiritually.

Suggested Books:

The Essential Guide to Healing, Randy Clark & Bill Johnson

ACTIVATION #7
FORGIVENESS BRINGS FREEDOM

And when you stand praying, if you hold anything against anyone, forgive them, so that your Father in heaven may forgive you your sins. But if you don't forgive, neither will your Father in heaven forgive your wrongdoing." Mark 11:25-26

In your anger do not sin: Do not let the sun go down while you are still angry, and do not give the devil a foothold. Ephesians 4:26-27

Forgiveness in a decision, not a feeling. God asks us to forgive because when we hold unforgiveness in our heart against someone, it creates a spiritual bond that cannot be broken until forgiveness takes place. God wants you to be free and in good health. Unforgiveness can open the door to the enemy and result in broken relationships, bad health, and depression, among other things.

Forgiveness doesn't signify that you have to trust the person. Neither does it mean that the other deserves it. It just shows that you are being obedient to God so that He can heal you, bless you and set you free from the situation and unholy ties that bind you to the person who wronged you. Forgiveness brings freedom.

Testimonies

Melanie: (from the Province of Misiones, Argentina)

"**I asked prayer for healing of my knee.** The doctors told me that they would have to operate. When Shari and the CDR kids prayed for me, nothing happened. Shari asked me if there was someone whom I needed to forgive, and I told her, 'Yes, I need to forgive my dad.' I made the decision to forgive him and when they prayed again for my knee, it was immediately healed! I returned to the specialist the next week and he told me I no longer needed surgery!

Later, God showed me that I had also treated my father badly, that our problems weren't just his fault, so I went to him and asked his forgiveness. He forgave me and God restored our relationship completely. So forgiveness brought me two healings!"

*Ceci, (age 13) was sitting by herself in the back of the church after the youth service where many teens had received the baptism of the Holy Spirit. Cata, a member of our national team, saw Ceci, just sitting there. As Cata was turning out the lights, preparing to leave, she approached Ceci, who appeared very sad, and asked her what was wrong.

"I want the baptism of the Holy Spirit so badly!" she said, "I need more of Him in my life."

Cata sensed that the Lord was prompting her to ask Ceci if she needed to forgive someone.

"Yes, I need to forgive my mom," she admitted. "She hits me when I go to church. I'm forbidden to come, but I have to come because that is where I learn more about my Jesus." She thought a minute. "And I need to forgive my youth leader because he's busy with university studies and doesn't have time to prepare lessons. There are times when we just play games instead of having Bible lessons, but that doesn't give me strength for the challenges I face in my home. I need to learn more about God."

"Are you willing to forgive?" Cata asked her.

Ceci nodded.

Cata guided Ceci in a prayer of forgiveness toward her mom and youth leader. Immediately Ceci began to pray in the Spirit, an unknown language flowing out of her mouth and joy filling her heart! Forgiveness had removed the spiritual blockage that had kept her from receiving God's promise.

*name changed

Matías was invited to speak at a youth camp and shared a teaching about forgiveness. Three months later he was invited back to the same church to give a devotional and re-connect with the same kids. Manuel approached Matías after the meeting to tell him that he had put into practice what Matías had taught. Manuel had gone to his father, asked forgiveness and reestablished their relationship that had been broken. One month later his father died unexpectedly! Manuel was extremely thankful that God had sent Matías to the camp with that message, just in time.

Activation:

1. Is there someone that you need to forgive? The Lord will help you because He knows that you will be free from the bonds that are between you and the other person. Forgiveness is not a feeling, it is a decision to obey God and leave the judgment in His hands. It is the only way to be free and healthy.

2. When you decide to forgive, tell God that you are willing to forgive _____ (the person's name) for _____ (whatever they did). The Lord will be with you during this process. Sometimes we need to forgive more than one time, but it is worth the pain for the freedom it will bring!

3. Ask God to fill that space in your heart where there used to be pain and unforgiveness with His love, peace and joy. Ask Him to fill you with more of His Holy Spirit.

4. Receive everything that God wants to give you and let Him affirm that you are his beloved child. Receive His love once again.

ACTIVATION #8
TAKING RISKS FOR GOD

Do you not know that you are the temple of God and that the
Spirit of God dwells in you?
1 Cor. 3:16 (NKJV)

Very truly I tell you, whoever believes in me will do the
works I have been doing, and they will do even
greater things than these, because
I am going to the Father.

And I will do whatever you ask in My name, so that
the Father may be glorified in the Son. You may
ask Me for anything in My name, and
I will do it. John 14:12-14

We show our love for Father God when we take risks in order to share His love with others. When we approach people to say that God loves them, or that He wants to talk to them, that He is seeking them out, or to ask permission to pray for their healing, we are more concerned about how to bring pleasure to God than the possibility of being mocked or rejected. And when we think this way, no matter how people respond, if we speak with love, respect and humility, we will leave godly fingerprints on their hearts. We have borrowed the phrase, "crossing the chicken line", that is used in BSSM*, to describe leaving our fear and comfort zone to take risks to bring God's influence into the situation.

*BSSM – Bethel School of Supernatural Ministry, Redding CA

Testimonies

Fernanda, 19-year-old EFX student,

"Before going into the projects (government housing) where we go to evangelize, while in prayer, I received the name, Marta, the color *black*, and *flip-flops*. When we went into that neighborhood I saw a woman in a store with a black t-shirt. I felt that I should go and share Jesus with her, and as we were walking toward her someone called her name. She was Marta! When I got closer I could see that she was wearing flip-flops! That created such faith inside my heart! I told her about the love of God. That day, Marta met Jesus and she understood that God has been thinking about her all the time."

Lucas and two EFX students approached eight high school students, who were waiting outside for classes to start. Five of them proclaimed themselves as atheists during the conversation.

Suddenly, Lucas said, "Hey, I'm going to prove that there is a God. Yamila and Gimena are going to listen to God and tell you what He says about you." The girls about had a heart attack when he said that, but quickly began listening to God while Lucas talked on a few minutes to give them some time to hear.

Yamila took a risk, a step of faith, and said to one of the boys, "I believe that God showed me that you feel lonely every night and you don't feel like you have any friends. Also, God knows your parents are having major problems, and He wants to be your father."

The young man's eyes filled with tears and Lucas quickly ushered him off to the side to talk privately so that the others wouldn't make fun of him. Later, when Lucas asked if they needed any more proof, everyone assured him that they didn't. They had just experienced the fear of the Lord in their lives.

Activation:

1. Ask God to fill you with His love. Take time to remember how much He loves you. Spend time receiving this love from God and worshipping Him.

2. Go out to share Jesus, staying attentive to the Holy Spirit. Pray in tongues, asking Him to show you who is ready for an encounter with God.

3. When you see the person, ask God how to start up a conversation and ask what is a problem that they are facing. Many times you won't know until you take a step of faith and start talking. Sometimes people will just open up and tell you what is going on in their lives and other times the Holy Spirit gives you information, or a pain in your body to show you where they are hurting.

4. Always treat the person with respect, love and humility. Let the Holy Spirit guide you.

5. The person is always more important than our agenda.

We want to show the love of God, not add another number to our list of converts. The goal is to love the person and with the help of the Holy Spirit, to help them have an encounter with Christ.

Suggested Reading:

The Risk Factor: Crossing the chicken line into your supernatural destiny, by Kevin & Chad Dedmon

Love Says Go, by Jason Chin

ACTIVATION #9
BREAKING LIES ABOUT FATHER GOD

See what great love the Father has lavished on us, that we should be called children of God! And that is what we are! The reason the world does not know us is that it did not know Him. 1 John 3:1

Jesus replied, "Anyone who loves Me will obey my teaching. My Father will love them, and We will come to them and make Our home with them. John 14:23

Satan is a thief and a liar. He wishes to rob us of our identity, purpose, health, family and any other valuables in our lives. One of the ways that he steals from us is by deceiving us with a lie. If he wants to rob our purpose, he tries to convince us that we cannot triumph, and that we are victims, poor, stupid, second-class or useless. If he wants to steal our identity he will try to persuade us that God is mad at us, that we are inferior, or that we always fail. Sometimes he uses someone else's mouth to insult, wound or put us down. If an authority figure mistreats, abandons or rejects us, it is easy to project that image on to Father God although He never did anything to deserve our fear, anger or distrust.

God is the perfect father that wants to love, protect, provide and communicate with His children.

Testimonies:

Alex, an EFX student:

"The Holy Spirit revealed to me a lie that I had been believing about Father God. He brought to mind a childhood memory of when my parents separated. When that happened, I began to believe a lie about Him, thinking that Father God was distant and that it was normal for a father to be absent.

As soon as God revealed to me what I was believing, I made the decision to renounce the lie. I asked Father God to exchange the lie for the truth. He did! He told me that He had always been beside me, and that He isn't like my earthly dad. He's a heavenly Dad who will remain beside me and never ever abandon me!

At that moment, God showed me a huge building that represented the lie I had believed which was demolished in a moment by His power. I never understood that a lie that I didn't even know that I was believing could grow to be so huge, but God leveled it in seconds with the truth."

Jeremiah, another EFX student:

"Many times I compared myself with other children of God and wished that I had what they did. I would look at myself and say, "I didn't have such loving parents, I didn't have the privilege to grow in that kind of surrounding. I didn't have covering or protection like my other friends in the church".

I constantly saw myself as inferior. I saw myself as poor, as a victim, and as down-trodden, someone who has all the factors against him and could never overcome. I feared future failures and didn't try to reach for excellence in my career choice, my Christian life nor in my relationship with others.

But Father God began talking to me about Him being my Father, and one day I got it! I am His son! He is a King which makes me a prince. I'm not second-class, or a victim! All of the lies dissolved like paper in water. They just disappeared. The feelings that had plagued me before changed into security, conviction and satisfaction! It was amazing!

Today I am learning how to behave like a prince, to honor, respect, and value myself and others. I am also learning to enjoy who I am and what Father God is doing in me—a unique work, valuable, personalized and unrepeatable. Thank you, Father!"

Activation:

1. Ask Father God to show if there is a lie that you are believing about Him.

2. Ask where/when you began to believe the lie?

3. If Father God shows you a specific situation, ask Him to show you where He was or what He was doing at that moment.

4. Forgive whoever taught you the lie.

5. Hand Father God the lie and ask Him what truth He will give you in exchange for it.[1]

Notes and Book Suggestions:

[1]De Silva, Dawna and Teresa Liebscher. *Sozo, Saved, Healed, Delivered: A Journey into Freedom with the Father, Son, and Holy Spirit.* Shippensburg, PA: Destiny Image, 2016. Print.

ACTIVATION #10
THE CULTURE OF HONOR (1)

"Honor your father and your mother, so that you may live
long in the land the Lord your God is giving you.
Ex. 20:12

Now we ask you, brothers and sisters, to acknowledge those
who work hard among you, who care for you in the Lord
and who admonish you. Hold them in the highest
regard in love because of their work. Live in
peace with each other. 1 Thes. 5:12-13

Honor all people. Love the brotherhood. Fear God.
Honor the king. 1 Peter 2:17 (NKJV)

The King will reply, 'Truly I tell you, whatever you did for one
of the least of these brothers and sisters of mine,
you did for me." Matthew 25:40

Every country has its own culture. The Kingdom of God also has its own distinct culture, and we call it the culture of honor. The Bible teaches us to honor our parents, our leaders and everyone else. Jesus modeled this culture in the way that he treated people. He received the children and blessed them. He treated the beggars and those rejected by society with love and respect.

He honored and respected women, even the prostitutes. When we show respect to our leaders, parents, teachers, schoolmates, fellow workers, employees, the homeless and treat them like Jesus would, we are living in the culture of honor.

Testimonies

Milagros (age 16, from the province of Misiones)

"One of my teachers came up to me at school and asked, 'Why are you different from the rest?'

I told her because I had an awesome God who lived inside me and that He made me different. My teacher didn't know who Jesus was as her family is atheist, so I explained who He is and what He did for us. Then I asked her if she wanted to experience God like I did. She said yes and received Jesus into her heart. She was very happy! God did all the work!"

Cami (age 15, ESN student, Buenos Aires)

"We decided to go out to eat after our church service. We received our food and had just sat down to eat when a security guard came to tell us that they were closing and we had to leave. So we got up, got our stuff together and made our way to the exit. Surprised, the guard approached us at the door simply to tell us 'thank you' for respecting him and his job. He told us that the majority of groups of teens and young adults, if asked to leave, wouldn't pay him any attention or would take forever to go. He was surprised that we got up so quickly, without complaint even though we hadn't finished eating. We wanted to be good representatives of Jesus."

Author's note. This shows the *culture of honor* in practice. May we all represent the kingdom in such an honorable way!

Matias, age 18 from the Patagonia of Argentina:

"When God called me to be a part of EFX, I had to put my plans of becoming an engineer on hold, which didn't bother me too much because I really want the life that God has planned for me. But me becoming an engineer was also my parents' plan. They are not yet Christians.

I told them what God had told me about going to EFX and their answers were a firm, "No! You have to study a career." They had already made up their minds that the following year I was going to start the University to become an engineer.

I tried to convince them with persuasion, with declaring that they had no right to decide my future because their plans didn't line up with God's plan for my life. But nothing worked.

Finally I decided to leave it in God's hands, for He had to be in charge of changing their minds in order for me to be able to go to EFX instead of the University. From that time on I set my mind to honor them, respect their viewpoint, and show them love and respect.

Months passed and the day came when I was accepted into the School of Extreme Formation. I gave my parents the news and their answer? "What date do you need to arrive?"

Activation:

1. Send a text expressing your thankfulness to three people:

a leader, a parent or relative and a friend. Tell them thank you for something specific like how they have made your life better.

2. Today, find one or two people outside of the church to whom you can show respect. It can include a store employee, bus driver, policeman, teacher or other. Tell them thank you for what they do and say something that will value, honor or respect them.

3. Ask God to help you learn how to cultivate the culture of honor in your own daily life.

ACTIVATION #11 — PROPHECY (1)

In the last days, God says, I will pour out my Spirit on all people.
Your sons and daughters will prophesy, your young men will
see visions, your old men will dream dreams. Even on my
servants, both men and women, I will pour out my Spirit
in those days, and they will prophesy. Acts 2:17-18

But the one who prophesies speaks to people for their
strengthening, encouraging and comfort. I Cor. 14:3

But he who prophesies speaks edification and exhortation
and comfort to men. I Cor. 14:3 (KJV)

What is prophecy? In it's simplest form, it is listening to God for others. 1 Cor. 14:3 tells us that the purpose of prophecy is to edify, exhort and comfort. Exhort, in the Greek, signifies encourage—not correction. People already know their faults; you don't need to remind them; nevertheless many times they do not know that God loves them fervently and can see their potential. Seek words of encouragement, words that will give believers and unbelievers alike hope. Words that will open people's hearts to God or tear down the lies that exist that are keeping them from a healthy relationship with Him.

Of course, every "word of the Lord" that we receive has to line up with what the Bible says; a prophetic word would never contradict the Word of God. The Bible is our standard. Since we are still in the process of learning, we teach our Castle kids and EFX students not to prophesy concerning spouses, callings, nor people having babies because if they hear wrong, they could cause hurt and confusion, the opposite of encouragement. Pray until you hear God's heart. Before giving the word (message) ask yourself, "Would I want someone to give *me* this word? Would it help or encourage me?" If it brings confusion, fear or feelings of inferiority, don't give it, most likely it didn't come from God.

If you believe that God is showing you that someone is passing through a difficult or painful time, ask God for a word that will strengthen, encourage or comfort that person.

Testimonies

The youth leader, *Teresa, was challenged to hear God before going out to evangelize at a bus terminal. When she bowed her head to listen, she saw the color purple, so when she left with her church group, after a training session with Kim, Shari and the students of EFX, she was looking for that color. When she arrived at the bus terminal, she saw a young lady sitting on a bench wearing a long purple coat. So Teresa sat down beside the girl and asked, "If I had a word of the Lord for you, would you be interested in hearing it?"

The young lady nodded and the Teresa had a moment of panic because as of yet she didn't have a word of the Lord to give. But just then, in her mind she saw the girl running toward the open arms of Father God and said, "I saw Father God with his arms wide open and you running into them."

The girl began to cry. "I'm backslidden," she confessed. "And

I wasn't sure that God still loved me."

Teresa prayed with the young lady to be reconciled with Jesus and invited her to be a part of their youth group. The girl told Teresa that she needed a church home and that she would be there the next Sunday.

*name changed

During a World Missions Summit, the Holy Spirit highlighted to Shari a young college student sitting in her seat during an altar call. Sensing that Holy Spirit wanted to encourage the young lady, Shari sat down in the empty chair beside her, leaned over and began to tell her that God wasn't fixated on her faults. He was focused on her potential, and that He was excited about all the awesome things that they could accomplish together if she was willing to let Him lead her life. Jordan began to cry as the Lord continued assuring her of His unconditional love and His wonderful plans for her life. Then Shari gave her a hug and left.

The next night, somehow in the midst of the six thousand students, Jordan found Shari and was able to tell her thank you, because she had been ready to give up, and God's reassurance was what she needed to continue on following Him with her whole heart.

·

One day, Chiemi and Becky entered a deli run by a married couple to buy a sandwich. After eating, Chiemi, who was always practicing receiving words of the Lord for others, approached the husband at the cash register and asked, "Excuse me, but do you have pain in your knee?

"No," came the response.

"Might your wife have pain in her knee?" Chiemi asked

again.

"I don't know. I'll ask her," he said, and went into the kitchen to bring her back out to the counter.

"Do you have pain in your knee?" Chiemi asked her.

"No... but I have terrible pain in my shoulder," the woman answered.

"We have seen our God heal many shoulders," Chiemi said, Can we pray that He heals you, too?"

The woman nodded. Chiemi and Becky prayed for her and she immediately was healed. Then they were able to tell her about the God who wanted to heal her.

***Authors' Note:** Although Chiemi gave an incorrect word of knowledge—God, who is so willing to help us reach people for Him, healed the woman anyway!

Group Activation:

1. Pair up with a person that you do not know very well.

2. When the leader indicates, everyone pray for the other person silently for one minute.

3. When the leader calls for your attention, each one should share with their partner how they felt led to pray.

4. Then they should ask their partner if it made sense to them or not. In this way, each can begin to learn how to distinguish the voice of the Lord from their own thoughts and opinions.

Activation #2:

1. Begin to pray for your family and friends.

2. Ask God to show you one person in particular. Ask Him to give you a word of encouragement for that person.

3. Send the person a text or a voice audio saying that you felt impressed by God to tell him/her _____, adding a scripture that you also received or other details that you feel would bless the person. Always share with love, respect and humility. Remember that your word must line up with God's Word.

4. Finish the message by asking the person if it makes sense to him/her ?

5. Usually people are thankful that you took the time to pray for them. Don't be offended if the person tells you that your word doesn't make sense. You are learning and the Holy Spirit needs to teach us how to discern between His voice and our own. At times, later on, the person may discover that it really was God speaking through you and other times we just missed it. That is why we must always maintain a respectful and humble attitude. We cannot fail if we take steps of faith motivated by love.

Note: A wonderful book that can help you grow in the prophetic gifts is *"Translating God,"* by Shawn Bolz.

ACTIVATION #12 — TREASURE HUNTS

I will give you hidden treasures, riches stored in secret places, so that you may know that I am the Lord, the God of Israel, who summons you by name. Isa. 45:3

Lay up for yourselves treasure in heaven... Matthew 6:20a

Many people think of treasure as being gold, diamonds, rubies, silver, and all kinds of precious stones. But God views people as treasure. He sees the dirty, the hungry, the fearful, the orphan, and His heart longs for each one to come into relationship with Him through Jesus' sacrifice on the cross. How does He reach them? By flowing through your hands, words, love, and actions so people can feel God's love through you.

Our teens are given treasure maps that have categories such as: clothing, name, location, colors/numbers, health problems and unusual things. These are our "treasure clues". We take time to wait on God, jotting down whatever we believe He might be showing us. Then we go and begin to evangelize in those areas, (plaza, mall, hospital,) and look for our "treasure clues". Obviously, this is not the only way to evangelize, and we share Jesus along the way, but when we find someone who matches what God showed us during prayer, our faith takes a leap and usually the results are glorious.

Testimonies:

Just before going to a new plaza to evangelize, the kids in the Summit gathered together to pray. Alejandra, (age 15) asked the Lord who she was supposed to talk to and immediately she saw a picture in her mind of a teen sitting on a park bench, surrounded by friends.

Upon arriving at the plaza, Ale quickly located the young man that she had seen in prayer, and taking another Castle teenager with her, she went to strike up a conversation with him. He was only half interested until suddenly Ale said, "Sergio! Why have you left the church?"

The kid jerked back and demanded, "How do you know my name is Sergio? And how do you know I left the church?"

Ale didn't have a clue how she knew! She was as surprised as Sergio was, but she quickly recovered and told him, "I didn't know, but God knows—and He wants you back!"

Sergio's eyes filled with tears, and Ale and her friend ministered the love of a heavenly Father to his wayward son.

Vicki asked the Lord to identify her ¨treasure¨ as she scanned the crowded mall. Suddenly, her gaze was drawn to a woman, and the Lord whispered, "Her legs need healing."

The woman sat down on a bench and Vicky approached her with a smile. Dropping down beside her, she asked, "Ma'am, did you know that Someone is thinking about you today? Someone who loves you and who died for you on a cross and knows everything that you are facing right now? You have a problem with your legs, right?"

The woman nodded, surprised, and added, "I've had a lot of pain for a long time, and in my hips as well. Also, I can't straighten my back while walking." Then she asked, "Do you mean to tell me that out of all these people, God sent you to pray for *me*?"

Vicki nodded and asked God to take all the pain away. Then, helping the woman up, they began to walk.

"There is no pain!" she exclaimed. The woman straightened her shoulders and walked upright, her eyes filling with tears. "I'll never forget what happened today!"

Activation: Hand out "treasure maps" to each one participating

1. Begin by inviting the Lord to come into the room. Worship attracts the Holy Spirit and opens our hearts to hear Him as well.

2. Ask the Lord to share His heart with you. He knows who is ready to hear the gospel. He knows people's heartaches, fears, pain and areas of vulnerability. Ask God to give you "clues" to be able to find these people.

3. Wait on the Lord. As words or pictures come to your mind, write them down on your "treasure map".

4. If you are in a group, everyone who received the *same locations* during prayer can divide into smaller groups and go together. It is a good idea for the members of each group

to share their "clues" with one another because sometimes the clues describe the same person. Also, group members can help each other find their "treasures".

SAMPLE TREASURE MAP

Suggested Book:

Love Says Go, by Jason Chin

ACTIVATION #13
REMEMBERING THAT GOD IS GOOD

*For the LORD is good and his love endures forever; His
faithfulness continues through all generations. Ps.100:5*

*Taste and see that the LORD is good; blessed is the one
who takes refuge in Him. Ps. 34:8*

*Every good and perfect gift is from above, coming down
from the Father of the heavenly lights, who does
not change like shifting shadows. James 1:17*

God is good. We must decide if we are going to believe what the Bible says about the character of God or what the world says. God gave mankind free will, which means that every human being has a choice to do good or evil. But when something bad happens, that comes from a bad decision made by a human, people want to blame God.

When our four children were still living with us, as parents we were in charge of the house, and yet, things happened of which we did not approve. If one of the kids hit another, took a sibling's toy, or began to argue, none of these situations were "our will", but they occurred because our children made their own choices. Sooner or later we would deal with the guilty party, and they would be disciplined. In life, people choose to make bad decisions that affect others, and it seems like God isn't paying attention. Don't be fooled; sooner or later justice will come. (Gal 6:7) Nevertheless, often the Lord deals with our character during the "waiting time". We can grow in faith, patience, love, joy and peace when we don't understand what is happening in our lives. This is when our faith is tested, when we are challenged in our belief that God is good in spite of the circumstances.

The Psalmist, David, understood the truth that God is good. It was a foundation in his life. Whether he was alone with the sheep, fighting against Goliath, fleeing for his life, reigning as king, or hurt by the behavior of his kids, in each situation, the truth that continually sustained him was that God is good. If this truth is a foundation in your life, come what may, your spiritual life will not waver. You will be like a solid rock, and after the storms blow by, you will remain with a good testimony that will last for all eternity.

Testimonies

When Jeremiah left his apartment to go to work, he realized that someone had stolen his car! At first, he was angry and frustrated, but then he began to pray for God to intervene. He and Bethany, his wife, are faithful in their tithes and offerings, and the Bible promises in Malachi chapter three that the Lord blesses those who faithfully give. In the end, the insurance agency paid Jeremiah even more than the stolen car was worth, allowing him to not only buy a newer car, but to buy four new tires as well. By believing God to take care of the situation, he came out better than he was before the car was stolen.

An eight-year-old boy was part of a group of kids who were taught on listening to God. After the time of waiting on God was over, he approached Shari, crying and said, "My aunt, whom I loved very much, died a few months ago, and I have been so sad ever since. But today, the Lord told me that she is with Him and that I shouldn't be sad anymore. He told me that I need to keep on going in my life and that I'll see her again one day." Then he smiled, radiating God's peace.

Malena, national team member, age 19:

"From a young age I went to church, together with my parents, and I loved Jesus. But **at age 12, my father made the decision to take his life.** I wasn't mad at God, but I began to believe the lie that perhaps He wasn't as good and loving as I had believed. It was a lie that I kept buried deep in my heart and never shared with anyone. But as time passed, God began to have personal encounters with me, which made me understand that He really is interested in each and every one of us. Perhaps we cannot understand everything that happens but today I know that He cares for me, loves me and has taken on the role of Father in my life.

The bad choice that satan influenced my dad to make and that the enemy planned to use to destroy me, God turned around. He gave me a testimony to encourage an orphaned generation and help them to be restored by the love of God.

I'm not a victim, I am an overcomer and can say with all my heart, GOD IS GOOD!"

Activation:

1. James 1:17 tells us that all good things come from God. Think of five or more good things that have happened to you this week. Write them down.

2. Think of five people (or more) that have blessed your life. Add them to your list.

3. Give thanks for everything that you have written on your list, each good thing/situation that happened this week and for each person that God has given you to bless your life.

4. Keep your list. Each week be attentive to the good things that happen, like when a family member cooks your favorite food, a gift, a great friendship, or a beautiful time alone with the Lord. Give thanks to God in the moment for the things He sent to bless you. You will see that Father God demonstrates His love to you in many different ways.

Notes and suggested books

Johnson, Bill. *God is Good; He's Better Than You Think.* Shippensburg, PA: Destiny Image, 2016. Print.

ACTIVATION #14
GRACE, YOUR SUPER-POWER

*For the grace of God has appeared that offers salvation to all people. It teaches us to say "No" to ungodliness and worldly passions, and to live **self controlled**, upright and godly lives in this present age. Titus 2:11-12*

*Let us then approach God's throne of grace with confidence, so that we may receive mercy and **find grace to help us in our time of need**. Hebrews 4:16*

*No temptation has overtaken you except what is common to mankind. And God is faithful; He will not let you be tempted beyond what you can bear. **But when you are tempted He will also provide a way out** so that you can endure it. 1 Cor. 10:13*

Grace is a supernatural power that helps us overcome our sinful desires, as the verses in Titus tell us. Grace gives us a higher standard than the Old Testament law. Jesus said, "the law says don't kill, but I say don't hate anyone. The law says don't commit adultery, but I tell you not to look at a woman with lust in your heart. (Matt. 5:27-28) The good news is that grace is a gift, a God-given force that gives us supernatural power to overcome sin.

When you are tempted to lose control, and to yell, gossip, fight, or disobey, you only have to call out to God saying, "Give me grace", and He is right there giving you the self-control that you need to avoid sinning. Of course, you still have a choice whether to use His Grace or not, but the Bible promises that He is faithful to help you walk above sin. There is no excuse to lose control of yourself if you know Jesus because He is willing to give you His supernatural power to conquer sin... it's called GRACE.

And how much did this super-power cost God? Why is it so important that you make good use of this gift? Because it was extremely expensive. It cost the life of Jesus!

Testimony

Karen, one of our national staff members shares this story:

"I had traveled many hours on a bus to be at a training weekend. I hadn't slept well on the over-night bus trip, but I was expectant of what God wanted to do in the lives of this group of teenagers. The church where the training was to be held was new to the ministry.

When we finished the first night of training at about ten in the evening, it was time to eat supper, but none of the leaders offered me any food. When I asked the main leader if there was any food left, he said, 'You didn't bring your own plate? Well, go ask the cook if she can find you one.'

One of the ladies of the church found me a plate and gave me some food. While I ate, everyone pulled out cushions and got ready to go to bed. I was getting frustrated and more so when they began to turn out the lights. I wondered where I was supposed to sleep when I realized that the leader was getting ready to go home to go to bed. I approached him and asked, 'Excuse me, where I am supposed to sleep.'

He shrugged. 'I don't know. We don't have a place for you. We didn't know that we needed it.'

Just then a castle girl came by and asked me if I wanted to use her cushion. I was so ready to tell the leader what I thought about him and his planning abilities, grab my stuff and go home. His leadership team had invited me! Just then I heard God's voice speaking, 'I brought you to this place. Don't leave.'

At that moment I prayed for grace, the force to do good, and His peace filled my heart. His grace helped me to speak graciously to the leader, giving him my best. And truthfully, I felt so much freedom in the Spirit. It was a really powerful weekend, and many, if not all, of the teenagers had awesome encounters with God."

Activation:

1. Read the three verses that are written at the beginning of this chapter.

2. Think of a situation where you lost control and fell into sin, (rage, gossip, pornography, bullying someone, or other sinful action).

3. Ask God to forgive you. Ask him to remind you to ask for His Grace *to help you in your time of need.* Romans chapter 6 will encourage you that you can overcome temptation

because as a Christian you are no longer slaves to sin. The apostle John also believed in your generation. 1 John 2:14b tells us that Christian young people are strong when the Word of God lives in them and that they have overcome the devil.

4. Ask God to help you make a plan to avoid situations where you have failed in the past.

5. Ask God about His willingness to help you conquer sin in your life. Write down His answer.

ACTIVATION #15
CREATIVE EVANGELISM

Then Moses said to the Israelites, "See, the LORD has chosen Bezalel son of Uri, the son of Hur, of the tribe of Judah, and He has filled him with the Spirit of God, with wisdom, with understanding, with knowledge and with all kinds of skills.... Exodus 35:30-31

In the last days, God says, I will pour out my Spirit on all people. Your sons and daughters will prophesy, your young men will see visions, your old men will dream dreams. Acts 2:17

The good news of Jesus Christ, his birth, life, death and resurrection, will never change. He is the Word of God in action. But the methods that we use to share this Good News must be very diversified because just one way to evangelize won't work with everyone. There are those who will receive a gospel tract, and others who won't. There are people who will listen to a street preacher, and others will just keep on walking. This is why we develop dramas and dances to be used with music containing a message. We also encourage kids and teens to draw or write cards with messages and Bible verses inside that show God's heart.

The Lord is very creative, and we are learning how to be guided by His voice, His Spirit and His gifts so that multitudes have an encounter with Him.

Testimonies

Lucas M., one of our national team members, was invited to teach a group of teenagers how to hear the voice of God at a local church. Then he explained that they were going to take some time to listen. The idea was that when the teens heard or saw a mental picture, they would write or draw what God was showing them. Afterward they would go to the plaza and try to find the person who God wanted to have the message. Lucas left paper in the middle of the table, and the teens listened in silence, waiting for God to speak. After a few minutes, they began to write and draw.

One of the boys, named Matías (age 13) drew a house in flames with a family with four children, the oldest being a girl, watching the house burn. Above the drawing he wrote *tree, depression, Marcos* and *suicide.*

Lucas glanced at Matías' paper and remarked, "It looks like you have a lot of people to find".

Matías shook his head. "No, it's all the same person," he answered.

Arriving at the plaza, the kids scouted the area for their "treasures," which were those who the Lord knew were ready for an encounter. Almost immediately, Matías saw a man leaning against a tree.

Approaching the man, Matías began his first attempt at evangelism with a direct question, "Are you depressed?"

The man was startled. "Why are you asking me that?"

"And is your name Marcos?" Matías continued.

The man's eyes widened, "How do you know?"

Matías showed Marcos the picture, "Did your house burn down?"

Tears filled Marcos' eyes. "Yes, ten years ago. My kids were there with us, watching it burn. And the oldest one is a girl, just like you drew.

Matías had one more question, "Are you thinking about suicide?"

When Marcos nodded, Matías told him, "You now have to accept Jesus into your life because obviously He showed me all these things because He knows and cares about you," and Marcos prayed to receive Jesus into his heart.

Jonathan, from the province of Entre Ríos:

"One Saturday afternoon, with my EFX classmate, Nadia, we decided to do treasure hunts with the kids in our discipleship group. It was the first time they had ever attempted anything like this, so we asked them to pray that God would show them what to draw or write. One seven-year-old girl drew a T-shirt with blue lightning rays and the words, 'God loves you!'

We went to a nearby plaza, looking for the person to whom she was supposed to give the card. Then we crossed paths with a guy wearing the same T-shirt that she had drawn! The little girl gave him the drawing and he was surprised when he looked at it, and was very open to hear what she had to tell him about God. He left that encounter knowing that God loved him.

Another boy (age 10) drew a heart on the outside of the card with the words, 'God will take care of you.' When he saw a man sitting alone on a bench he ran up and gave him the card. When the man looked at the card, he got all choked up, his eyes filled with tears and he told the group that he had just received the diagnosis that he had cancer. He had never known God, so when they presented the way of salvation, he accepted Jesus as his savior. I felt like I was supposed to give him a hug, and he told me that he felt loved and knew that God was going to take care of Him."

Activation: You will need paper, colored pencils, crayons or markers.

1. Ask God to give you His heart for the people that are ready to have a relationship with Him.

2. Ask God to give you clues to help you find them.

3. Wait and listen.

4. Draw what the Lord shows you. Write the words that you hear.

ACTIVATION #16
BREAKING THE LIES CONCERNING JESUS

*I no longer call you servants, because a servant does not
know his master's business. Instead, I have called you
friends, for everything that I learned from my Father
I have made known to you. John 15:15*

*Greater love has no one than this: to lay down one's life
for one's friends. You are my friends if you do
what I command. John 15:13-14*

Jesus left heaven to show us how to live like a child of God
with the power of the Holy Spirit. He died on the cross to
pay the price for our sins and open up a way to God so that
we may know Him as Father. When we repent for our sins
and ask Jesus to be the Lord of our lives, we enter the family
of God. It's like getting his last name and all the benefits
of being his children come with the package. Now that we
have access to Him, He gives us power to overcome sin, to
rescue lost souls and to walk with Him in the supernatural.

But satan fears us developing an intimate relationship with
Jesus. The enemy tries to impede our relationship from growing
with God by putting lies about His character and how God sees

us into our minds. At times we can't hear God's voice or believe His Word because we are too busy believing these lies. They may sound like: "Jesus is mad at me. I'm not important. He's busy. He doesn't care about me." If we accept these lies, our spiritual growth is stunted. But if we uncover his lies, renounce them and ask Jesus to show us the truth, we can restore our communication with Him and grow in relationship, in the Word and in our faith.

Testimonies

Gastón shares his story:

"Ever since I was little, my relationship with other guys wasn't good. I tried to make friends, but it just didn't work. I thought maybe it was because I didn't have a dad or a brother. I finally got tired of trying to find a male friend. Because of my experience I thought that Jesus was the same way, that he thought I was different or weird too. I began to think I always had to do something in order to win the friendship of others.

In one of the EFX classes, I asked Jesus to show me what lie I was believing and where He was when I first believed it. Immediately, I saw Jesus walking beside me, but I was unaware of His presence. I felt him speak to my heart and say, 'If you look at me and stay focused on the fact that I am right beside you, you will believe that I *want* to be your friend.' He assured me that he wasn't seeking out my imperfections but that he loved me and enjoyed spending time with me. At that moment I saw Him smile at me. Everything changed in my life when I stopped believing the lie and began to believe the truth. Now I have friends all over the country, guys and girls, and I have no doubt that I am loved and am learning to see myself as Jesus sees me."

Carolina, leader of Club Castillo:

"I was born into a Christian family. I came to know the love of God at age twelve at my first training weekend of CDR, and I have served Him ever since in whatever way I could. A few months ago, in an open class of EFX, the topic was the love of Jesus and how he accompanies us daily and changes us from the inside. I was shocked to realize that I hadn't been thinking of Him as so present in my life. I was always conscious of His sacrifice on the cross, but I had forgotten about his daily companionship and how He sees me.

So I asked Jesus where He was during the most difficult moments of my life, and I broke down and cried to see Him there, right beside me, always beside me! He showed me that he has always been close, and knowing that gives me such security! **Jesus wants my friendship, not just my service, but my heart.** Understanding that he never left for even a second, even in the most difficult times, has given me a greater security to walk as a beloved daughter of God and to enjoy a deeper friendship with Jesus".

Activation:

1. Ask Jesus if there is a lie that you are believing about Him.

2. Ask Jesus where or when you learned the lie.

3. Ask Him where He was or what He was doing at that time.

4. Ask Him to reveal to you the truth of the situation.

5. Forgive whoever taught you the lie or caused you pain in this memory.

6. Ask Jesus to forgive you for believing the lie about Him. Renounce the lie.

7. Ask Him to replace the lie with the truth and to fill you with more of His Presence.[1]

Notes and Book Suggestions

[1]De Silva, Dawna and Teresa Liebscher. *Sozo, Saved, Healed, Delivered: A Journey into Freedom with the Father, Son, and Holy Spirit.* Shippensburg, PA: Destiny Image, 2016. pp. 55, 94.

Activation #17 — The God-nudge

One day Peter and John were going up to the temple at the time of prayer—at three in the afternoon. Now a man who was lame from birth was being carried to the temple gate called Beautiful, where he was put every day to beg from those going into the temple courts.

When he saw Peter and John about to enter, he asked them for money. Peter looked straight at him, as did John. Then Peter said, "Look at us!" So the man gave them his attention, expecting to get something from them.

Then Peter said, "Silver or gold I do not have, but what I do have I give you. In the name of Jesus Christ of Nazareth, walk." Taking him by the right hand, he helped him up, and instantly the man's feet and ankles became strong.

He jumped to his feet and began to walk. Then he went with them into the temple courts, walking and jumping, and praising God. Acts 3: 1-8

The lame man was at that temple gate *every day,* but one afternoon, when Peter was passing by the temple, he felt a "nudge from God". Looking at the man, suddenly Peter's faith level rose and he declared healing over the man. Many times, a "God-nudge" comes as a thought, a challenging idea, or an impression that is easy to ignore. But if we are attentive, with our spiritual ears turned toward God, we can learn how to distinguish between those God-nudges and our own thoughts.

Don't be afraid to take a risk. God loves a good adventure, too. Look how Jesus responded when Peter asked if he could get out of the boat and walk on the water. Jesus loved it! So even if you mistake your own desire to approach someone for His God-nudge, He gets involved anyway because he loves to back up His kids. And if we get rejected, He is there to give us a hug.

Testimonies

Esteban came to the Summit ashamed of his past. From ages 12-16 he had been addicted to drugs, but came to Jesus the year before and joined Castle ministry. During the "hearing God" workshop, he was challenged to listen to the Holy Spirit on the street. So the same day, in downtown Buenos Aires, when he saw a kid about his age, he felt God pushing him to share his testimony. So he did.

The young man shook his head, ashamed, and said, "I am also addicted to drugs, and I want to get out." Esteban introduced his new friend to Jesus. and they prayed together.

Later Esteban shared that God showed him that he wasn't less of a son because of who he used to be. ***God didn't measure him by his past, but by being His son.***

Milagros, a young teen from the Misiones province, felt very insecure about praying for sick people but wanted to step out in faith even though she was afraid. One day, at school, a friend began to feel very sick and the school nurse diagnosed her with dengue fever, which had turned into a plague in that area with over 60,000 cases reported at one time. The nurse quickly left to call the girl's father to come and get her.

Milagros saw her friend waiting for her dad, summoned her courage and asked, "Can I pray for you?" The friend was very timid, so Milagros prayed quickly so as not to embarrass her.

Immediately, her friend felt something go through her body, and she asked, "What did you do to me?"

Milagros answered, "Jesus healed you!" They called the nurse who confirmed that ALL of the symptoms had disappeared! She was completely well!

Activation:

1. Ask the Lord to help you sense His God-nudges in order to see the opportunities that he is setting up for you to share His love with someone for salvation, healing or to give a Word of encouragement / knowledge.

2. Go out with a sense of expectancy, attentive to His nudges.

3. Write down your adventure with God.

Note: The more you pray in the Spirit, or wait on the Lord, the more opportunity you are providing for God to set things up for you. Isaiah 64:4 says that God works on behalf of the one who waits for Him, and Paul said that he prayed in the Spirit all the time. (1 Cor. 14:18) Look at the adventures Paul had and the impact he made on the earth!

ACTIVATION #18
THE POWER OF THE TESTIMONY

*The men of Ephraim, though armed with bows, turned
back on the day of battle; they did not keep God's
covenant and refused to live by His law. They
forgot what He had done, the wonders He
had shown them. Psalm 78:9-10*

*They triumphed over him by the blood of the Lamb and
by the word of their testimony; they did not love their
lives so much as to shrink from death. Rev. 12:11*

The root of the Hebrew word, "testimony" signifies "do it again, duplicate or repeat." When you tell a testimony, you are raising the faith and the expectations of others so that they can also experience God's love, power and healing.

Testimonies

Camila and Alex, two EFX students, were sharing Jesus with a group of teens in the plaza. A classmate had a word of knowledge that someone was suffering back pain and one of the kids reluctantly admitted it was him—but no, he did not want prayer. The students smiled and began to tell healing stories that they had seen in the last few weeks. Suddenly a look of surprise crossed the teenager's face. He stood up and exclaimed, "What happened to my back? The pain left!"

Cami and Alex asked the young man to try something that he couldn't do before, and he made some movements that before he couldn't do without being in excruciating pain. He was shocked that God had healed him while listening to testimonies!

"The Lord healed you!" exclaimed Cami, "Now can we pray for you?"

This time he said yes. There is power in the testimony!

Ceci, age 19 from Neuquén shares her testimony:

"My pastors and leaders challenged me to take more responsibility in ministering to the youth in my church. They believed that I could disciple younger teens. In my heart, however, I felt incapable and was afraid that I would let everyone down, so I asked God to use someone else. I loved the teenagers, but I just didn't feel like I was good enough to help them get closer to Jesus.

A few days later, I went to a CDR camp in another town. I was hoping God would speak to me through a word of knowledge or during the ministry times. I knew God could talk to me if He wanted to do so. While there during a free period, I began to chat with another leader from another church who began to tell me her testimony. It was exactly what I had been experiencing! She talked about how she felt like God was pushing her to do something that she didn't feel capable to do, but that when she took the step of faith, He was right there to help her. Without realizing it, this other leader was confirming the decisions that I was supposed to make. I began to cry and God took away my fears, assuring me that He was sufficient."

Activation: Experiencing the power of the testimony

1. Make a list of experiences where you have seen, experienced or heard of a situation where God intervened. It can be salvation, healing or deliverance from fear, depression, witchcraft or anything that is not from God.

2. During the next few days, look for opportunities to share one of these testimonies with someone that God shows you needs to hear it. If you have a testimony where you saw someone's knee healed and you find someone who needs a healing in their knee, share that testimony with them, and then ask permission to pray for them. Take a step of faith with the Holy Spirit.

Group Activation:

1. Ask the people in the group to think of healing testimonies that they have experienced.

2. Choose someone to give his/her testimony. Then, ask the group if someone there suffers from the same problem. Ask the person who shared the testimony to pray for the

one who is suffering, along with whoever else who wants to join the prayer. Choose others to also share and do the same thing afterward. If it is a large group, various groups can be praying at the same time.

3. Ask how many received healing. Let those that just received healing give a testimony, giving glory and thanks to God. Be sure to thank God for every healing, miracle and testimony.

ACTIVATION #19— WAITING ON GOD: OPEN THE DOOR TO THE SUPERNATURAL

Those who wait on the Lord shall renew their strength; they shall mount up with wings like eagles, they shall run and not be weary, they shall walk and not faint.
Isa. 40:31 (NKJV)

For since the beginning of the world men have not heard nor perceived by the ear, nor has the eye seen any God besides You, **who acts for the one who waits for Him**. *Isa. 64:4*

There are various promises made to those who wait on the Lord in Isaiah 40:31. One is that they will have their strength renewed for the many daily opportunities and challenges they face. They are also promised a different viewpoint. A flying eagle can see what is happening over a large area while those on the ground are limited by what they can see because of all the physical obstacles surrounding them such as mountains, trees, or buildings. In the same way, when we wait on the Lord, he raises us up to see His viewpoint, which looks very different from our limited one.

And just as an eagle can see what is up ahead, sometimes God will show us what will happen in the future. And finally, we will run and walk with spiritual strength to complete our daily tasks.

Isaiah 64:4 states another promise, every bit as powerful as the first. We are told that *God acts for those who wait on Him.* This means that when I spend time in God's presence, waiting for Him to speak to me, Bible in hand, heart and ears attentive to His voice, He acts on my behalf. Whether I hear anything or not, the time is not spent in vain because I am assured that God is working for me be it in my family, my job, my future, or disarming traps of the enemy. It isn't easy to wait, but we will wait for things that are important to us. Let's show God that He is important to our lives and take time to wait on Him.

Testimonies

A teen from the Patagonia tells us:

"In the CDR camp in Puerto Madryn, Shari taught us the ways that God speaks to us and then gave us time to wait in His presence. At the beginning, nothing happened, but as I waited, eyes closed, I saw God with His arms wide open. I couldn't see His face because it shone too brightly, but He came up to me like a friend and suddenly kneeled down in front of my feet. I thought, no! God would never kneel in front of me!

But then I realized that he was washing my feet with such love and tenderness. I remembered the last supper when he washed his disciples' feet, serving them. I then understood that He was showing me how He was and still is. He always has his arms open to us, waiting for us to come to him at any time, and we should be loving servants, carriers of the faith and heirs of the promises of His Word."

Roberto, from Cordoba, had a desire in his heart to be a part of the EFX school in Buenos Aires, but it looked totally impossible, so he gave up his dream. Two weeks before the school began, Roberto attended a CDR camp. In his own words he shares:

"During a time of waiting on the Lord, God talked to me about fulfilling my dreams, goals and much more. In that moment my desire to go to EFX returned, stronger than ever. The following day, having heard of my encounter with God and my strong desire to attend EFX, the director of the school informed me that there was an opening. The Lord changed the heart of my parents who aren't Christians yet, and spoke to my pastor and other key people in my life. A week later I was on my way to the school."

During a training weekend in the Patagonia, **the Pastor's wife of the church stopped in to see how everything was going.** She and her husband had gone through a lot lately that had left her feeling spiritually empty and dry. Worship music was playing and everyone was quiet, waiting on the Lord, so she decided to wait on the Lord, too. "Holy Spirit, what do you have to tell me?" she asked.

Immediately a song dropped into her spirit. She wrote down the lyrics and memorized the tune that she heard in her head. Not only was it a beautiful song, but it brought an intimacy with God, along with His peace and a refreshing to her that she hadn't experienced in a long time.

Activation: Make yourself comfortable, with Bible and notebook beside you. Put your phone aside on silent.

1. Spend time thanking God for being so good.

2. Ask Him to cleanse you from every sin, mistake and doubt.

3. Tell Him that you are waiting for Him. This is His time.

4. Wait. Listen. Write or draw whatever He shows you.

Activation #20 — Breaking the Lies about the Holy Spirit

Nevertheless I tell you the truth. It is to your advantage that I go away; for if I do not go away, the Helper will not come to you; but if I depart, I will send Him to you. John 16:7

However, when He, the Spirit of truth, has come, He will guide you into all truth; for He will not speak on His own authority, but whatever He hears He will speak; and He will tell you things to come. John 16:13

For those who are led by the Spirit of God are the children of God. The Spirit you received does not make you slaves, so that you live in fear again; rather, the Spirit you received brought about your adoption to sonship. And by Him we cry, "Abba, Father." Romans 8:14-15

Who is the Holy Spirit? He is the part of God that always accompanies, guides, loves and corrects us. He brings conviction of sin in order to keep us from falling into the traps of the enemy. He helps us to share our faith and "cross chicken lines". He has many adventures planned for our lives should we choose to partner with Him.

Jesus gave us the promise that He wouldn't leave us alone but would send us the Holy Spirit to guide us into all truth. When we receive Jesus as Savior, His Spirit brings us into relationship with Him. But when we receive the baptism of the Holy Spirit, our capacity for his presence and power greatly increases. Satan plants lies in our minds so that we won't even want this promise from the Father because the devil knows that the baptism of the Holy Spirit will give us power over the kingdom of darkness. When we receive more of the Holy Spirit, we also get His authority, gifts and power over sin.

Testimonies

Fernanda, (age 19)

"In my heart it was hard to believe that I could ever have a strong relationship with the Holy Spirit. Truthfully, I really thought that He was too holy to hang out with me, that He could have a deep relationship with others, but not with me. This was the lie that was hidden in my heart. During the activation of uncovering the lies, I decided to ask the Holy Spirit what He thought about me. I decided to break every lie that said I wasn't able to have a deep relationship with Him. The best thing that happened is that He told me that he loved spending time with me and that he had been working out all the details of my life up until the present. He said He was willing to hang out with me all the time and that we could go on adventures together! I felt so happy being able to enjoy a great relationship with the Holy Spirit and to be secure in the idea that He loved spending time with me as well."

Camila, from Villa Regina in the Patagonia:

"In an encounter with God, I asked if I was believing a lie

about Him. He said yes, that I was believing that I could never be 100% full of the Holy Spirit. I began to think about it and God, as usual, was right. The lie was believing that if I wasn't 100% full of the fruit of the Spirit, that if I got angry or thought badly about someone, then the Holy Spirit didn't want to use me, or couldn't ever use me in the gifts.

I asked His forgiveness for thinking He expected me to be perfect. I was limiting Him from allowing His power to flow through me. Obviously, He still needs to work in my life, but the fact that I am a work in progress won't keep me from asking Him to fill me with His power and presence every day and from having adventures with Him."

Activation:

1. Ask the Holy Spirit if there are lies that you are believing about Him.

2. Ask him where or when you learned this lie. Forgive whoever taught you the lie.

3. If the Holy Spirit shows you a specific situation, ask him to show you where He was or what He was doing at that moment.

4. Ask Him to reveal the truth of the situation. Exchange the lie for this truth.[1]

Notes and Suggested books

[1]De Silva, Dawna and Teresa Liebscher. *Sozo: Saved, Healed, Delivered: A Journey into Freedom with the Father, Son, and Holy Spirit.* Shippensburg, PA: Destiny Image, 2016. Print.

ACTIVATION #21
BRINGING HEAVEN TO EARTH

Let your kingdom come, and Your will be done, on earth
as it is in heaven. Matt. 6:10

Do not be afraid, Little flock, for your Father has been
pleased to give you the kingdom. Luke 2:32

As you go, proclaim this message: "The kingdom of heaven
has come near." Heal the sick, raise the dead, cleanse
those who have leprosy, drive out demons. Freely
you have received; freely give. Matt. 10:7-8

When you don't know what the will of God is, think about what the Bible says. Jesus prayed for the kingdom of God to come to the earth. What does that look like? Matthew tells us that healing the sick, casting out demons, and raising the dead are the results of what happens when the Kingdom of God shows up on earth! Jesus prayed, "Let Your will be done on earth as it is in heaven." Is there cancer in heaven? Is there pain in heaven? Is there abuse in heaven? Of course not! We need to renounce and rebuke sickness, evil spirits and demonic situations in the name of Jesus. Let's work with God to fulfill the words of Jesus in order to bring heaven to earth.

Testimonies

Roberto remembers the first time that he discerned the voice of God through a physical impression:

"I was with my EFX classmates visiting a group of teenagers one Saturday at a local church. I began to chat with a ten-year-old and out of the blue, my back started aching. The Lord had never spoken to me in this way before, but finally I asked the kid if he had pain? He told me, yes, in his back. When I asked him how bad it was, he told me it was about a eight on the pain scale of 1-10. When I prayed for him, the pain disappeared from his back and from mine at the same time!"

Cami *(Alberti, suburb of Buenos Aires)* **was on a train** with her team when the woman behind her got a phone call that left her in tears. When Cami asked if she could help, the woman told her that her husband had just had a second heart attack in the hospital where he was a patient and wasn't expected to survive. Cami began to tell her that nothing is impossible with God and asked if she and her friend Abby could pray with her. The woman nodded and the girls began to pray a prayer of faith for the healing of her husband.

After prayer, Cami gave the lady a tract with the church's address on it. She looked at it and said, "If my husband survives, we will come and visit your church to thank you for your prayers."

Nine months later a woman showed up at Cami's church holding a tract in her hand. At the beginning of the service, when the pastor asked if anyone wanted to give thanks for something, the woman stood up. She recounted what had happened on the train and said, "Now I want to show you something." She went out of the church and came back with her husband in tow.

"He is completely well," she said, beaming. Neither she nor her husband had any religious beliefs. They were more agnostic than anything else. But when the pastor gave an altar call, both went forward to receive Jesus. She now testifies to being happier than she has ever been in her life.

Kevin, member of national CDR team recounts:

"One day we called a meeting of all of the teenagers who were leaders of their castle teams in the Buenos Aires area. The objective was to take a day to seek God's presence, fill up on His love and then go into the public to demonstrate His power.

After spending time in His presence, listening, waiting and asking Him to fill us with His love for people, we went to one of the busiest transportation centers in Buenos Aires. One teenager, Lucas, from a little church in a very humble neighborhood, was desperate to see God's power poured out in public. While evangelizing, he saw a man on crutches who said his name was Tito.

Tito told us that he had been on crutches for 14 years and was in much pain. Lucas prayed for him and Tito began to move his legs, walking slowly at first and then gradually running, crying and shouting thanks to God for his miracle.

The people who were waiting for the subway as well as others who had just arrived, had seen Tito running back and forth, crying and shouting, and they all wondered why the man was crying so hard. They began to gather around to see what was going on. Then, Lucas, taking advantage of the crowd of people pressing in, explained that Jesus had just healed Tito, and began to preach about how to know this awesome God who loved people so much! Over a dozen people prayed and accepted Jesus as their Savior that day!"

Activation:

1. Think about a situation that is not lined up with heaven. If you aren't sure, ask yourself, are there sick people in heaven? Is there unforgiveness, sadness, or hatred in heaven?

2. Begin to take authority in prayer over the situations that are not lined up with the kingdom of heaven. Pray like Jesus prayed in Matthew 6:10, asking the Lord to let His will be done in these situations *as it is in heaven.* Jesus is our model.

3. Give God thanks for listening and answering your prayers. You are praising and thanking Him in faith and that brings much pleasure to the heart of Father God. (Heb. 6:11)

ACTIVATION #22
HEALING: GOD'S WILL

*Jesus went through all the towns and villages, teaching in
their synagogues, proclaiming the good news of the
kingdom and healing every disease and sickness.
Matthew 9:35*

*Very truly I tell you, whoever believes in Me will do the
works I have been doing, and they will do even
greater things than these, because I am
going to the Father.   John 14:12*

*Philip said, "Lord, show us the Father and that will be
enough for us." Jesus answered: "Don't you know Me,
Philip, even after I have been among you such a
long time? Anyone who has seen Me has seen
the Father. How can you say, 'Show us
the Father'?"   John 14:8-9*

If you want to know what our heavenly Father is like, you have
to study the life of Jesus. The whole Bible teaches us about
God but Jesus is the exact representation of the Father. (Heb.
1:3) Therefore we must take our healing doctrine from the
life of Jesus. When we study the life of Jesus, it is obvious that
healing is His will. Jesus healed all the sick that came to him.

He never said, "God is forming your character with this sickness, therefore I'm not going to heal you."

Neither did He say, "Your faith is too little so I'm going to let you stay sick."

Some Christians may say these things but this theology doesn't come from Jesus. When someone approached Jesus with little faith, Jesus healed his son. When someone came with great faith, He healed her daughter. When a man said, "If you want to, would you heal me?" Jesus answered, "I want to!" and healed him.

Testimonies

Recounted by Fernanda, an ESN student,

"One day, some students of ESN went to McDonald's, and while in line, one of us received a word of knowledge that someone had an injured knee. When we saw a girls' volleyball team seated close by, nine players and two coaches, we believed the word was for one of them. We asked them if someone had a knee problem, and they told us that the girl whose knee was injured was part of their team but wasn't there today. So we asked if anyone else had an injury and one of the girls told us that she had hurt her shoulder. Her pain level was an 8 on the pain scale of 1-10. We prayed three times, until the pain totally disappeared. When the team members saw that, they asked us to come to their tournament the following weekend to pray for the team since there were many injured players and they kept losing.

Arriving at the Club that next weekend, we began to cheer for their team, and they won that game! When it ended, they invited us over to pray for their injured players. Many got healed!

One girl, named Guada, was in constant pain from a dislocated kneecap. The Lord healed her instantaneously! Her parents were so impacted by her healing that they came the next weekend to meet the students from ESN. Guada's mother told me that when her daughter arrived home she couldn't stop doing two things, crying and running up and down the stairs!

Her father had a cyst on his own knee, so we prayed for him. Afterwards, he couldn't find the cyst, so we encouraged him to do something he couldn't do before. There was a slight discomfort, but we are believing that God will complete His work. Guada's dad told us that he wanted to come back to faith in God.

We continue to minister to this team on the weekends and are believing for a mighty harvest to come forth out of what God is doing in the lives of the players and their families!"

Activation:

1. Find someone who is sick. Before praying for the person, remember that Jesus already paid the price. Ask what the problem is. If they have pain in their bodies, ask them on a pain scale from 1 to 10 how much pain they are experiencing (1 is low, 10 is high). Use this method to measure what is happening when you pray. When the pain level drops, the faith level rises.

2. Pray for the person, short and simple. Many times Jesus only spoke a word or a phrase, and the person got healed. Afterward, ask if the person felt a change or not. Ask him or her to test it.

3. Don't be afraid to ask permission to pray again. Jesus prayed twice for the blind man. Matt. 8:24

4. Rejoice in what God does. Thanking him brings more of His presence and healing. If you didn't see a healing in the moment, that doesn't mean that it won't happen in an hour or the next day. Assure the person that God loves them.

ACTIVATION #23 — INSPIRE OTHERS

Don't let anyone look down on you because you are young,
but set an example for the believers in speech, in conduct,
in love, in faith and in purity. 1 Timothy 4:12

Do not store up for yourselves treasures on earth, where
moths and vermin destroy, and where thieves break in
and steal. But store up for yourselves treasures in
heaven, where moths and vermin do not destroy,
and where thieves do not break in and steal.
Matthew 6:19-20

We want to live our lives in such a way as to provoke others to go after adventures with Jesus. No matter your age, you can influence others to love, honor, heal and share their faith. The Holy Spirit wants to guide you and help you maintain a good testimony in order to inspire others.

Testimonies

Ursula, age 62, went to the bank to get her social security check. An older lady sat down beside her, complaining of severe pain in her knees. Ursula thought to herself, *what would those Castle kids do in this situation? They would talk to the woman* *about God and then pray for her healing.* So Ursula decided to do the same.

She began to talk about Jesus and asked the woman if she believed in Him. The old lady nodded and said that she was Catholic. Then Ursula asked her if she believed that Jesus loved her and could heal her. The old lady answered, "Yes, my priest says the same thing."

Ursula asked permission to touch her knee and pray for healing. The woman had very little faith that something would happen but said yes anyway. So Ursula asked Jesus to heal the knee. Thinking about what the Castle kids did after praying for someone, she said to the old lady, "Now, stand up and try it out."

The old lady stood up and took a few steps. A surprised look came over her face, and she began to exclaim, "It doesn't hurt! It doesn't hurt any more!" She was so happy!

A bank security guard came over to investigate. "What happened? What's all the noise about?"

"Everything is good," the two ladies assured him. When he realized what had happened, he was amazed as well!

"I crossed the chicken line today. I took a risk for God," Ursula told me, beaming. "Just like the Castle kids! God is faithful to me, too!"

Flor, EFX student:

"Mondays are free days for EFX students, so every Monday I take my nephew, Nicolas, age 10, to school. We always walk, singing, inventing praise songs and have a good time. When I started EFX, my evangelism teacher challenged us a lot, so I began to do the same with Nico, saying, 'Nico, I challenge you to cross the chicken line!'

At first, it was hard as he was very nervous, but after praying for many people, kids and adults alike, someone got totally healed of back pain.

The next Monday after I picked him up, we sat down on the bus, and he said to me, 'Aunt Flor, can we preach to someone?'

I looked at him, sleepy-eyed and with absolutely no desire to do anything other than get him to school, but he insisted enthusiastically, 'Can we cross the chicken line again?'"

Activation:

1. Ask God to give you His love for people.

2. Ask Him to help you to see the opportunities that He is giving you. Ask for the courage to take risks for Him and show His love through prayer for whatever need surfaces.

3. Go out into the public: mall, grocery store, park, etc. with eyes and ears attentive, listening for the Holy Spirit's guidance. When you see someone and believe that God is highlighting that person, approach him/her with courtesy, love and humility. Strike up a conversation, being interested in what the person has to say. Listening to people conveys that you care about them. *God gives us opportunities to minister to people when love is our motivation.*

4. Do the same thing with your grandmother, little brother or niece. Invite someone in your life to come on an adventure with you and the Holy Spirit.

ACTIVATION #24
THE CULTURE OF HONOR (2)

*For just as each of us has one body with many members, and
these members do not all have the same function, so in
Christ we, though many, form one body, and each
member belongs to all the others.   Romans 12:4-5*

*If one part suffers, every part suffers with it; if one part is
honored, every part rejoices with it.   1 Cor. 12:26*

As was stated in the prior lesson on the culture of honor, this is a culture that treats every person like Jesus treated people when He walked the earth. But there is much more to this culture. We are the body of Christ, and in a healthy body, every member works together in order to complete a purpose. There is no room for competition because everyone has a role to complete. The culture of honor recognizes the gifts of each one and celebrates the victories of others as if it were their own. The reality is that when one member of the body wins, everyone benefits. There is no competition or division in heaven, nor in its culture. Each time that one of our brothers or sisters achieves a victory, it is a win for the entire body of Christ!

This means that if I want a position in the church but it is given to someone else, I must be happy for that person. I need to celebrate what God did in that person's life, not pouting because I didn't get it. If I pray for the healing of someone and they do not get healed, and afterwards a brother in Christ prays for the same person and healing comes, what should my response be? If I understand the culture of honor, I will celebrate the healing as if it were the answer to my prayer, or better yet, as if I were the one being healed! Your victories belong to your team, and the victories of others in the body of Christ, are yours as well. When we understand how to live in the culture of honor, we will advance the kingdom of God on the earth faster than ever!

Testimonies

Rich was a successful pastor who was so hungry for more of God that he left his church of sixteen years to move, together with his wife and kids, to attend a ministry school on the other side of the country. The Lord opened up part time work for him in the janitorial department while he studied since he'd had some unexpected economic challenges. However, after he finishing the school, the Lord instructed him to stay on as head of maintenance for the school and church installations.

His classmates, with no previous ministerial experience, were chosen for key positions that Rich was qualified to occupy, and Rich had to choose to rejoice for them, congratulate them and assure them that they were the best people for the jobs.

Years passed, and Rich came to the point where he told the Lord that he would stay on permanently as the head of maintenance and janitorial services if that was God's best for him.

Soon after, he was offered a full-time job as Bible professor for that same school of ministry.

Note from the authors: Rich came and ministered in both schools here in Argentina and left an enormous impact on the students. His humility and transparency marked every student that he touched and he taught us all how to walk in the culture of honor.

Activaction:

1. Think about when someone gained a position or promotion that you wanted. Or think about when someone received an answer to prayer and even though you had been praying just as hard for the same thing, you didn't get your answer.

2. Begin to thank the Lord for what happened to the other person. Celebrate what God is doing in his/her life. Do it out loud. Celebrate as if it were your own victory.

3. If there is something in you that doesn't want to celebrate the other person's victory, ask God to forgive you for that attitude and help you change your heart.

4. Ask the Lord to help you learn how to live the culture of honor on a daily basis.

ACTIVATION #25
TALKING TO GOD: PRAYER

*And pray in the Spirit on all occasions with all kinds of
prayers and requests. With this in mind, be alert and
always keep on praying for all the Lord's people.*
Ephesians 6:18

Pray continually.
1 Thes. 5:17

God, the creator of the universe, wants to communicate
with us! And if that isn't enough, He wants to listen to
what we have to say, too! He is interested in what we think,
in our dreams, our ideas, even in our problems. Psalms 139
says that His thoughts about us are more numerous than
the grains of sand on the beach. You are very important to
God. And you have a very important place in His kingdom.

Everything good that happens on earth is tied to prayer. James
1:17 says that every good and perfect gift comes from our
Father God. But how? Through the prayers of His kids. The
apostle Paul tells us, "pray without ceasing". That means that
we should continually be listening, attentive to the thoughts
that God gives us, so that our prayers can stay connected to

His heart, bringing His will to earth. Your prayers have a lot of power. You can change the world, one prayer at a time.

Testimonies

Lucas C.'s passion was soccer. Years of arduous training, practices, exercises, games and sacrifices had finally paid off. After seeing him play, a scout from the country of Turkey made him an offer to go there to play professionally. The benefits included a house, a car and a considerable monthly salary. For a seventeen-year-old, whose objective in life was to play professional soccer, it seemed like the answer to his dream. That night he went to church and slipped into the back row. He only had a couple days to sign the contract, and Lucas said to God, "If you have a different plan for my life, tell me now."

Immediately the Lord baptized Lucas in the Holy Spirit, and he began to pray in tongues. He felt an inner fire and a transformation on the inside. At that moment the dreams of God for his life became the only thing important to him. Lucas gave up professional soccer and began to have Holy Spirit adventures. Now he is pastoring and influencing the lives of many young people. He's never regretted leaving the other life behind because this one is so much better.

At age 18, Rachel was preparing to leave Argentina, where she had lived during her teenage years, and return to her birth country in order to study and reconnect with her grandparents, uncles and cousins. She loved the Lord and was serving as a leader in CDR, ministering to teenagers. During an event, there was a prayer vigil and her turn to be involved was from four to five o'clock in the morning. Everyone was praying over the Argentine map and receiving words of the Lord for the various regions. Just then, Rachel heard the Lord asking her to give up her birth country and everything that she had planned for her future. She felt like He was asking her to stay in Argentina, calling her to work with the youth of the country. She tried to discern if this was God or her own thoughts, thinking maybe she could wait until after college to come back and serve.

Suddenly, the other leader, David, who had no idea what was going on inside of Rachel, stood up and said, "When the Lord speaks, you have to obey now and not put it off until later." Rachel knew that the Lord was speaking to her through David's words.

After receiving three more confirmations during the next few weeks, Rachel gave up her own plans in order to fulfill God's calling on her life.

Authors' note: Rachel and Lucas eventually fell in love, married, and are now jointly pastoring youth and young adults in Buenos Aires, along with their little son, Noah, (our grandson).

Activation:

1. Begin to praise and worship the Lord. Give Him thanks because He is willing to listen and speak to you. Ask Him to cleanse your heart and if there is any sin, repent quickly and receive his forgiveness.

2. Speak to Him about the things that weigh heavy on your heart; needs, family problems, or character flaws. Pray in

your own language or in tongues. If you write down your prayer requests, leave a space next to it where you can add the answers and miracles when they come.

3. Ask God what are the burdens that are heavy on His heart. Write down what He says. Pray over them.

Optional Activation:

1. With your leaders, set up a prayer vigil. It can be for 2-4 hours or all night long.

2. Take time to put together prayer topics for the event.

Examples: Names of unsaved friends and family, ethnic groups in your city, challenges your city is facing, maps and pictures of missionaries, or flags of other countries.

3. Expect that God is going to pour out His presence over the meeting. Music can be playing in the background to create a worshipful atmosphere that sets the stage for worship, prayer and intercession.

ACTIVATION #26
LIVING AS JESUS LIVED

*Those who say they live in God should live their lives
as Jesus did.* 1 John 2:6 (NLT)

...because as He is, so are we in this world. 1 John 2:17b

Obviously if God gives us promises like the ones above, He believes that it is possible for us to fulfill them. How did Jesus live? He lived in victory, walked in authority over the enemy, had self-control, was never deceived by sin and always walked in the supernatural. Our inheritance is to *"live like Jesus lived in this world."* Jesus knew the Word, prayed to the Father, was baptized in the Holy Spirit and utilized the gifts. And He loved to teach others to live the same way.

Testimonies

Gastón and David went to the plaza and saw a young man sitting on one of the benches. The boys approached him and struck up a conversation, learning that his name was Nahual. When Gastón mentioned God, Nahual told him that he was an atheist and didn't believe in that "God-stuff". Gastón continued a friendly debate with Nahual while David just listened, but suddenly David noticed that his right wrist had begun to ache. Having learned that sometimes the Lord lets us feel others' pain in order to minister to them, David took a risk. "Does your wrist hurt?" he asked.

Nahual's eyes grew wide, "How did you know that?"

David shrugged, "God showed me. It's your right wrist, isn't it?"

Nahual just nodded, totally shocked that a God who didn't exist could communicate.

"Can I pray for your wrist?" asked David. "What do you have to lose?" Nahual agreed and David and Gastón prayed that all pain would leave in Jesus' name.

"Okay, move it around and tell me if there is a change or not."

Nahual moved his wrist and his mouth dropped open. "It doesn't hurt! How did you do that?"

"I didn't," David responded. "God did."

Nahual didn't pray the sinner's prayer that day, but he definitely had some thinking to do about how a God who doesn't exist can talk and heal people. And David exchanged phone numbers with Nahual, believing that one day he will want to know more.

Antonella's testimony:

After performing an evangelistic drama in a plaza, one of the castle girls, Antonella, approached a woman who was watching and began to share with her the love of Jesus. The woman began to cry and told the girl that she had tried to kill herself that morning and couldn't do it, but had it all planned out to go through with it that night. As Antonella assured her of God's love and intervention the woman began to cry. She decided that she wanted to know God personally, too, and accepted Jesus as her Lord and Savior and felt the desire to die lift off of her. Now she has life because she has Jesus.

Activation:

1. Ask the Lord to give you opportunities to share His love with others.

2. Go out into the public and find someone with whom you can share the love of Jesus. Ask permission to pray for their needs or health.

3. Bless a neighbor or a stranger in a practical way. For example, you could rake leaves, sweep their porch or sidewalk, pick up garbage in front of their house, or any such helpful work.

4. Write down what you did and what results it produced. Whether the person gets saved or you just brought a smile to his/her face, when you walk in love God can work through your actions! Share with your group what happened.

ACTIVATION #27 — PROPHECY (2)

In the last days, God says, I will pour out my Spirit on all people.
Your sons and daughters will prophesy, your young men will
see visions, your old men will dream dreams.
Even on my servants, both men and women, I will
pour out my Spirit in those days, and
they will prophesy. Acts 2:17-18

But the one who prophesies speaks to people for their
strengthening, encouraging and comfort. I Cor. 14:3

But you can all prophesy in turn so that everyone may
be instructed and encouraged. 1 Cor. 14:31

When a child is outside the sound of his father's voice range, at times the father will ask one of the other children to carry a message. The child carrying the message is not better than the child who receives it, but was in a better position to hear at the time. This is a picture of prophecy, when Father God wants someone to know something, that for some reason they cannot at the time hear for themselves. When we learn how to hear God's voice, we can enjoy hearing Him not only for things that pertain to ourselves, but to help others connect to His heart as well.

The prophetic gifts are a bridge between God and others. To people who are disillusioned by the church or closed to the opinion of other Christians, a word of prophecy or knowledge can change everything, and show that God is interested in and seeking after them. If you give a word of God, with an attitude of love and humility, (example: "I believe that God is showing me...") people won't feel threatened, but loved by God. Unfortunately, there have been those who have used the prophetic gifts to manipulate, steer, and punish those who are not in agreement with them. That is not the true prophetic because it doesn't flow from a heart of love, and God is love.

May the Lord raise up a generation that can discern between the true words of God and those that are actually the opinions of the messengers. This last days generation needs to know how to use the gifts of the Spirit to connect the atheists, the backslidden and the disillusioned to God's heart. We need a generation that walks in intimacy with the Holy Spirit and developed in His gifts. We need a generation of people who have learned how to discern God's voice from their own and who are willing to take risks to see hearts, bodies and lives healed and restored by God's Spirit.

Testimonies

Alejandra, during a missions trip to the Patagonia.

"God showed me in prayer a dark-skinned woman, and I heard the word, 'guilty'. I found her while out sharing Jesus and shared with her what the Lord had told me. The woman began to cry and confessed that she felt guilty for the death of her son. Right there she accepted Jesus as her Savior and felt the presence of God."

Natalia (part of CDR national staff) **was in charge of teaching a group of children how to hear the voice of God,** finishing up with a short time of waiting to hear Him speak. Afterwards, each child was given a piece of paper with which they could make a cube, and within the cube they could draw or write a message for the person that would receive it. Upon finishing, the kids accompanied Naty, the pastor and a few others who also went along to share Jesus, to a city park where they were to give their cubes to the person indicated by God.

Manuela, (7 years old) felt impressed to give hers to a woman who happened to be talking to the pastor. She approached her, handed her the cube, and said, "This is for you. I believe that God wants you to have it."

The woman took it, opened it and began to read the message inside, which was scrawled in big letters, "You need to come back to God. My momma left the church, too, and everything went bad until she came back to God. Now I'm happy."

"Who knew? Who wrote this?" the woman demanded, looking at the pastor.

The pastor had no idea since he wasn't aware of the classroom exercise, and asked the little girl.

"I wrote down what God told me to write." Manuela told him.

The woman was shocked. She knew that God has spoken to her that day and did so through a little seven year old.

The EFX students decided to enter one of the most

infamous neighborhoods in Buenos Aires to share the gospel of Jesus Christ. When Adrian approached a group of his friends that were talking to some of the local guys, suddenly pain shot through his knee.

"Anyone here have pain in their knee?" he asked the group.

"My knee doesn't hurt but I walk with a limp," one of the neighborhood guys said.

"Can we ask God to take away your limp?" asked another student. When permission was granted the students prayed for healing. When the young man walked around to see if there was a change, he, along with the whole group, was amazed to see the limp had completely disappeared!

Activation:

1. Begin to pray for your friends and family members.

2. Ask God to show you one person in particular. Then ask Him to give you a word of encouragement for him/her.

3. Send the person a text or an audio message telling him that God showed you _____, adding a Bible verse that you sensed that he/she needed to receive and/or other details that you believe God is giving you for that person. Always share the word with a loving attitude, respect, and humility.

4. Finish by asking the person if what you sent made sense.

5. Usually people are very thankful that you took time to

pray for them. Don't be offended if they don't understand *in the moment* how your word relates to their life. You are learning and the Holy Spirit will teach you how to discern between His voice and your own opinion. Sometimes, later on, they may realize that God really did give you something that applied to their life—and sometimes we just miss it. That is why we must always maintain a respectful and humble attitude. We cannot fail if we love people because they will be impacted with God's love during the encounters.

Optional activation for evangelism:

1. Spend time praying for the people that you will encounter on your outing and begin to listen to the Lord.

2. If you hear something, write it down.

3. Go looking for the person or people that the Spirit highlights and start a conversation. If you didn't hear anything specific, that's okay, just go out and look for someone that you can talk to anyway. When you feel like the Holy Spirit is giving you the opportunity, share what He gave you. Sometimes you may get an impression, a word, or feel a pain in your body **after** starting a conversation with someone.

ACTIVATION #28
HEALING: JESUS IS OUR MODEL

Heal the sick, raise the dead, cleanse those who have leprosy, drive out demons. Freely you have received; freely give. Matthew 10:8

And Jesus went about all Galilee, teaching in their synagogues, preaching the gospel of the kingdom, and healing all kinds of sickness and all kinds of disease among the people. Matthew 4:23 (NKJV)

For those God foreknew He also predestined to be conformed to the image of His Son, that He might be the firstborn among many brothers and sisters. Romans 8:29

Jesus is our model. He came to earth not just to reconcile us to God, but also to show us how we ought to live. Looking at the life of Jesus, we see the importance of miracles and healing. Jesus always went around healing sick people! He taught and preached, but there was always a demonstration of power that accompanied His words.

The world needs to see an authentic representation of Jesus. When you gave your life to Jesus, the Holy Spirit began to live inside of you to transform you into His image. In the same way that children take after their parents, we ought to become like Father God. Jesus, as the firstborn, showed us that healing the sick should be part of our daily lives. Healing the sick is part of our inheritance that we receive as children of God, no matter our age.

Testimonies

Nadia and Evelyn were sharing Jesus in a poor area in the center of Buenos Aires when they stopped to talk to a lady. Evelyn told her that God loved her, and that she was a princess in His eyes, very special to His heart. Nadia asked if she could pray for any need that the woman might have. The woman nodded and told the girls that her knee was in a lot of pain. When the girls asked her where her pain level was on a scale between 1 and 10, she told them that she was at a 15! The girls prayed a short prayer and then asked if there was any change.

"I felt something running up and down my leg," came the answer.

Nadia and Evelyn explained that God was healing her. They prayed two more times and then asked her to try to do something that she couldn't do before. The woman began to walk, back and forth, perfectly! Her limp was gone!

Afterwards, she accepted Jesus as her Savior. She wanted to know this awesome God who loved her enough to set her free of all pain!

One day, Heidi began to chat with a woman in the plaza who brought up the fact that she had a sore knee. Remembering that Lucas V. had received an impression from God that he was going to meet someone that day with a sore right knee, Heidi called Lucas over. When Lucas prayed for the lady, she was instantly healed. She was so excited, and began to walk back and forth without her cane! Afterward she wanted to know Jesus personally.

"One more thing," the lady said, "can you also pray for my neck?

"Of course." Lucas began to pray, "Papa, would you please heal..."

"Papa? You call God, Papa?" the lady interrupted.

Lucas and Heidi assured her that, yes, God wanted to be her Papa, too. Those who have repented of their sins and received Jesus as Savior can call God, "Papa". Jesus paid the price of our sins so that we could now be sons and daughters of God!

The woman left soon after, saved, healed and content to be in relationship with Papa God.

Activation:

1. Find someone that needs a healing. Ask what the problem is.

2. You already know how to pray for a sick person. Ask the Lord if there is another way that He wants to heal this time. If not, pray as before. Jesus healed by the guidance of the Holy Spirit. Ask the Holy Spirit how He wants to heal this person.

3. If there is any doubt that God wants to heal, study the following verses:

Isa. 53:5	1 Peter 2:24
Prov. 4:20-22	Matt. 4:23
Psalm 103:3	Matt 10:8
Psalm 147:3	Mark 16:18

And there are many more. You can write them down as you find them.

ACTIVATION #29
SERVANT EVANGELISM

*For even the Son of Man did not come to be served, but to serve
and to give His life as a ransom for many. Mark 10:45*

*Now that I, your Lord and Teacher, have washed your feet,
you also should wash one another's feet. I have set you an
example that you should do as I have done for you.
John 13:14-15*

Jesus told us that the greatest in the kingdom of God was
the servant of all. One way that we can show God's love is
to serve others. There are people who do not want to listen
to a sermon, nor wish to debate if there is a God or not—but
hardly anyone has an argument against an act of kindness.

Testimonies

When asked how they could serve, the municipality of
Mendoza invited a group of Castle kids to paint the public
school. While the teenagers worked, the neighbors passing
by couldn't help but notice the number of kids, dressed in red
T-shirts who were painting the school. Curious, the neighbors
began asking who they were, where they were from and why
they were working.

There were so many people interested that when the team finished up their paint job, they presented their first public presentation of the gospel (through dance, drama and an invitation to know Jesus) in the main plaza. Many of those curious neighbors were in attendance and interested in their message after seeing them serve the community.

Some years ago, in San Antonio Oeste, in southern Argentina, a big evangelism event was planned that would last a couple hours in the main city park. Teens came from a neighboring province to help out the local CDR team with dramas, choreographies, human videos and teenagers preaching short messages in between. At that time, there was a lot of occult influence over the municipality, and it was very hard to get permits for Christian public events. But although the permits were granted by the municipality a couple of weeks in advance, the day before the event, they were revoked! At first, everyone was angry and frustrated, but then as the pastors and youth leaders began to pray, the Lord gave them a different strategy.

The next morning, everyone arrived at the municipality asking for brooms, rakes and shovels. All of the castle kids, more than seventy, wearing their red T-shirts, began cleaning the parks and streets of the city and painting curbs. And they did it with big smiles on their faces!

Many people wanted to know what was going on, until even the local radio station showed up and began interviewing the kids, asking them why they were cleaning the streets and plazas. The kids told them that it was because they loved Jesus and wanted to bless the people of the city.

Because of their servant attitudes, the group had more opportunities to share their faith in Jesus—including over the radio—than they would have by giving two hours of dance and drama in the city park! Plus, their community work grabbed the attention of some key people and opened up opportunities for them to give presentations in the local schools in the weeks following!

Group activation:

1. **Think** of ways that you can serve in your house, church, and community. Remember, this blesses God's heart to see you acting like Jesus.

2. As a group, **choose** activities in which you can serve your church. Make a plan.

3. **Complete** your plan with joy and energy.

Individual Activation:

1. Think of something that you can do to be a blessing to someone in your family. Do it for the family member and also to bless the heart of Jesus.

2. Share with your group, afterward, how you served your family in order to encourage others to do the same.

Activation #30
Conquering Fear

God has not given us a spirit of fear, but of power and of love and of a sound mind. 2 Timothy 1:7 (NKJV)

So do not fear, for I am with you; do not be dismayed, for I am your God. I will strengthen you and help you; I will uphold you with my righteous right hand. Isaiah 40:31

I have given you authority to trample on snakes and scorpions and to overcome all the power of the enemy; nothing will harm you. Luke 10:19

Faith is the spiritual force that brings the Kingdom of God to earth and moves mountains. Its counterpart, fear, activates hellish forces that can paralyze people from moving into their God-given destiny. Your greatest enemy can be a fear of failure, a fear of the unknown, or a fear of taking risks, all which will keep you from believing the promises of God and entering into your destiny.

Can we overcome fear? Is it possible for a timid person to change and replace the fear with faith and courage? Courage is not the absence of fear, but taking action in the face of fear. In the Kingdom of God, we are called to tread upon snakes and scorpions, both of which represent the demonic realm, and exercise power over the enemy in order to rescue people from the kingdom of darkness. We have been given the Word of God and the infilling of the Holy Spirit to accomplish this, but with all that God has given us, we still have to make the decision to leave our comfort zone and overcome fear.

How? We conquer fear, not by emotion or will-power, but by inviting the presence of the Holy Spirit into our lives and then obeying His promptings. His presence gives us confidence to enter into the territory of the enemy and bring hope, truth, healing and deliverance to those bound by lies. The world is looking for answers that you, empowered by the Holy Spirit, can give if you push past your fears. On the other side of fear is a testimony.

Testimonies

Sara was afraid to stay alone. Every time that she would have to stay by herself, caring for her younger sister or cousins, a profound fear would grip her. She began to beg the Lord to rescue her from the fear, and He taught her that Jesus won the victory over the enemy using the Word of God. So, to build up her faith, she began to memorize verses such as 2 Tim. 1:7, Luke 10:19 and Isaiah 41:10 and to say them out loud when she began to feel fear. Sara learned that she had authority over the spirit of fear and could rebuke it in the name of Jesus. Between quoting the Word and the name of Jesus, the fear would flee. It couldn't stick around.

Rubén, age 16 from Buenos Aires tell us:

"On Friday I was in school, and I had been asking God for the chance to preach during a free period to a friend. On Thursday He gave me two hours, but I did nothing because I was afraid. On Friday, again, He gave me two free hours, and the first hour I did nothing. God spoke to me and said, 'I am giving you these free periods. What will you do?'

I was determined to do it. While listening to a worship song with my ear-buds in place, I started watching my classmates. God gave me a burden for them. I went to the blackboard and pulled up a chair. With my heart beating almost out of my chest, I stood up and began to preach to all the kids in my classroom.

Then a girl asked me, 'How can I get God to forgive me?' That question opened up the door, and I led them in a prayer of salvation. Around 14 kids gave their hearts to Jesus!

When I got down off the chair and went to my seat, half of the kids gathered around me and wanted me to continue talking to them about God. I told them how I came to Christ and how God had used me. One of the girls shared that she experienced a miracle this last year, and she began to cry as she told what happened. This created a great expectancy in the classroom. I thank God that many teens heard the message. **If you push past your fear, you can find an awesome victory."**

Activation:

1. What are you afraid of? Is it keeping you from completing your God-given destiny?

2. Fear is your enemy. It walks with worry and is sent by the devil to rob you of your faith, peace and joy.

3. If you have given your life to Jesus and have repented for your sins, you can be free of fear because fear comes from the enemy, and you don't have to take anything from him.

4. Ask the Lord to show you how the fear entered into your life. Did you experience something traumatic? Are you believing a lie? Did you watch a horror movie or demonic series on television?

5. Once you discovered where the fear entered, you can close that door in the name of Jesus. If you watched or touched something that opened the door, ask Jesus to forgive you and then command the fear to leave in His name. If you made an unholy pact, renounce it in the name of Jesus. If you are in a correct relationship with Jesus, the fear will have to leave your life.

6. Begin to worship God. Tell him how awesome He is. Ask Him to fill each space of your life with the Holy Spirit. When you are full of the Spirit of God, nothing fearful or demonic can torment you. Greater is He (Jesus) that is in you than the devil that is in the world, (1 John 4:4).

7. Memorize Bible verses that will remind you of your authority over fear. Luke 10:19, Isa. 41:10 and 2 Tim.1:7 are just a few that will help you to walk in courage.

ACTIVATION #31
THE POWER OF THE HOLY SPIRIT

*Nevertheless I tell you the truth. It is to your advantage that
I go away; for if I do not go away, the Helper will not come
to you; but if I depart, I will send Him to you.*
John 16:7 (NKJV)

*And if the Spirit of Him who raised Jesus from the dead is
living in you, He who raised Christ from the dead will
also give life to your mortal bodies because of His
Spirit who lives in you. Romans 8:11*

*God anointed Jesus of Nazareth with the Holy Spirit and
power, and how He went around doing good and
healing all who were under the power of the
devil, because God was with Him.*
Acts 10:38

Jesus chose twelve disciples so that they could learn how to bring the kingdom of God to the earth. Not only did He teach them, but He also gave them authority and power to heal the sick, cast out devils, cleanse lepers and raise the dead. When Jesus returned to heaven, He sent the Holy Spirit in order to teach His disciples how to continue bringing His kingdom to earth. We can also have adventures with the Holy Spirit every day.

Testimonies

Ceci, a teen from Neuquen Province:

"About a month ago, during my personal prayer time, God showed me a girl who was worried about sickness but felt too sinful to ask God for help. I wrote down what God showed me, and I saved it in an envelope in order to give it to her when God pointed her out.

Two days later I was in a park and I began to talk to a lady who told me that her husband was sick and that she was really worried about him. I felt like she was the one who God had spoken to me about so I gave her the letter, along with my phone number so that we could stay connected. I explained to her how God had laid her on my heart, and she began to cry.

The following day she sent me a text asking how to get to my church. The next Saturday she came to our young adult service and gave her life to Jesus. Today, she, her husband and little girl are faithfully attending church and are thankful of how God radically changed their lives. God is good!"

Belén (from Cordoba) and Ruth (from Misiones) EFX students:

"**We had a free day.** We decided to go down to the center of Buenos Aires. On the way, we gave ourselves a challenge to talk to one person about Jesus. It went so well that we decided to pass the entire day sharing Jesus with people and praying for their needs.

We talked to approximately sixty people that day, between the two of us. It was crazy! God gave us specific words. Many people gave their hearts to Jesus, and we even ended up going into a bar and talking to a person who had the night before tried to commit suicide!

God guided us to each person that day. We enjoyed ourselves so much, and it was good because we wanted to do it. The love of God for each person compelled us that day."

Activation:

1. Ask the Holy Spirit what testimony He wants to give you this week.

2. Ask the Holy Spirit what He wants to teach, show or tell you. Wait and listen.

3. Write or draw what you hear.

4. Obey what you hear the Holy Spirit say. He will never tell you anything that is against the Bible. He will also sound like Jesus, because it is His own Spirit.

Evangelistic Activation:

1. Go out into a public place and be attentive to the voice and guidance of the Holy Spirit. Have an adventure with Him.

ACTIVATION #32
BE LIGHT IN THIS WORLD

When Jesus spoke again to the people, He said, "I am the light of the world. Whoever follows Me will never walk in darkness, but will have the light of life." John 8:12

You are the light of the world. A town built on a hill cannot be hidden. Matthew 5:14

In the same way, let your light shine before others, that they may see your good deeds and glorify your Father in heaven. Matthew 5:16

*Every good gift and every perfect gift is from above, and comes down from the **Father of Lights,** with whom there is no variation or shadow of turning. James 1:17 (NKJV)*

Think about how the light changes the atmosphere of a dark room. When the light is turned on, the darkness doesn't swallow it. Rather, the darkness flees and the light takes its place because light is more powerful than darkness. If we stay "plugged in" to the Light of the World, Jesus, He will convert us into lights, that can affect our homes, schools and communities. The key is to stay permanently connected to The Light every day, reading the Bible, talking to Him, spending time with Him and receiving His love and affirmation.

Testimonies

Hearing the whisper of the Holy Spirit, Sabrina (age 17), shared Jesus with a middle-aged woman at a bus stop in her home town. The woman responded by asking to receive Jesus into her life. Two weeks later, Sabrina heard that the woman had died! She was so glad that she had obeyed the nudge of the Holy Spirit!

Jeremiah and Jonathan met a twenty-five year old man. After introducing himself, Jonathan told him that Jesus loved him and that God was thinking good things about him. *Marcelo began to tell them that he used to minister in a church, had fallen into temptation, had lost his son, had lost his job and was frustrated and hurt. The boys talked to him about Jesus' love and told him their testimonies of God's forgiveness and grace during the difficult times in their own lives.

Marcelo gave them permission to pray for him, and during the prayer, Jeremiah received a word of knowledge. He said to Marcelo, "Hey, I sense in my heart that although the devil has wanted to destroy your life, God wants to do something new. That something that you thought was completely destroyed and impossible to fix, He is going to take it and make it new and beautiful.

Marcelo was shocked! His eyes filled with tears and he told them that Jeremiah really had heard God—that Marcelo had recently separated from his wife and couldn't think of anything else.

Jonathan and Jeremiah finished by assuring Marcelo that they would continue praying for him and be there to accompany him on his faith journey. They exchanged phone numbers and invited him to come to church with them.

Evelyn (17 years old) chose the topic of God for her debate in English class. After she turned in her paper, she asked her philosophy professor for her opinion. The teacher confessed that she had never seen God portrayed as a loving father before. Evelyn began to feel pain and fear, and realized that the Lord was showing her how her teacher felt. She later approached the teacher, gave her a hug and began to pray for her as the Lord showed her. The teacher ended up giving her heart to the Lord!

Activation:

1. Remember that you are light in your church, home, school, work, university, etc.

2. Go out to share Jesus, radiating his love. Smile at people. If you see a need, find out how you can help. If you see a person who needs prayer, ask permission to pray for him/her.

3. **Be light in your home:** If there are dirty dishes in the sink, wash them, or put them in the dishwasher. Sweep the floor. Take out the garbage. Find ways that you can show God's love to your family.

4. Pray that God shines through your life. Use your words and your actions to attract people to Him and make the world a better place.

Activation #33 — Being vs. Doing

As soon as Jesus was baptized, He went up out of the water.
At that moment heaven was opened, and He saw the
Spirit of God descending like a dove and alighting
on Him. And a voice from heaven said, "This is my
Son, whom I love; with Him I am well pleased."
Matt. 3:16-17

We love Him because He first loved us. 1 John 4:19 (NKJV)

But God demonstrates His own love toward us, in that
while we were still sinners, Christ died for us.
Romans 5:8

Before Jesus did a miracle, preached a message, or did any kind of ministry, the Father loved and affirmed Him. The Father loved Him because Jesus was His son.

When our kids were born, immediately we fell in love with them. When we adopted Jonathan, our third child, at eight days old, the same thing happened. As each child joined the family, the love in our hearts increased and wrapped around them. Although our babies could only cry, eat and dirty their diapers, we loved them with all of our heart. And in spite of the fact that they didn't wash the dishes, clean the house, cook a meal or earn money, it didn't matter because they were ours. As they got older, they learned how to return our love and began to do things for us that we didn't even require, just because they wanted to make us happy.

God is the same. The Bible says that everyone that accepts Jesus as Savior and Lord is a son and daughter of God. Good parents love their kids, and God is the best Parent of all. Therefore, when we serve him, we don't do it to gain his love and favor. We already have it! We set up chairs at church, let others go before us, tell Bible stories in the nursery and clean the bathrooms because we love Him and His people. We don't have to win His love; we work with Him *because* we love Him and want to bring joy to His heart by acting like Jesus.

Testimony

Becky, director of EFX and ESN:

"In my first year at BSSM in California, God began to work on my identity concerning "being vs. doing". I was raised in a Christian home where we always were part of a church. I sincerely loved God and wanted to please Him with my life, but I was constantly frustrated. I felt like I wasn't doing enough to receive God's approval. If I read the Bible for a half an hour, I felt bad for not having read it for an hour. If I prayed for twenty minutes, I felt like I should have prayed longer. If I fasted three days or ten days, it never felt like enough. No matter what I did, I felt like I always fell short of some invisible standard.

Before Jesus started his ministry, God said something

amazing, 'You are my beloved Son, in whom I am well pleased.' In these few words, God declared identity, love and approval. Jesus was established in His identity as God's Son, and received His love and affirmation BEFORE He did anything noteworthy: before doing a miracle, preaching a sermon or completing His mission on the earth.

The first time I heard this message, it changed my perspective, but it took time to figure out how to live it out day by day. I learned that as a daughter of God, before reading the Bible, spending time in His presence, fasting or praying, I already had His affection and affirmation. When I woke up each morning knowing that God already loves me and He's proud of me, I noticed that I really enjoyed reading the Bible and spending time with Him. I wasn't logging in my time, I was just enjoying time with my Heavenly Dad.

With the exception of Christianity, all religions in the world have a common denominator: it's all about what one has to **do** to reach or please a god. For us it is different. Our God did everything possible to reach us and provide what we needed in order to be His children. Now I don't have to work to earn His love, instead I live out of His love. First, I **am** a beloved daughter in whom He is well pleased. This is my basis of everything I **do** for Him."

Activation:

1. Spend five minutes thinking about what you do.

2. Determine why you do what you do. Are you completing these activities to earn God's love? Are you afraid that He

won't love you if you don't do them?

3. Put on worship music, and make yourself comfortable. Ask God to show you how much He loves you. Meditate on Him loving you just because you are His child. Listen to His heart and receive His love.

4. Decide to serve God because you love Him, working with Him to complete your various activities.

Note: If you cannot connect with God, check your life for unconfessed sin, or ask Him if you are believing a lie.

• If there is sin blocking your communication with God, repent and tell Him you are sorry. Receive His forgiveness and start over. God wants to show you how much He loves you.

• A lie of the enemy can also hinder your communication with your heavenly Father.

• Ask Him what lie you are believing, rebuke the lie and ask God to show you the truth.

Activation #34
Closing Doors to the Enemy

Truly I tell you, whatever you bind on earth will be
bound in heaven, and whatever you loose on
earth will be loosed in heaven. Matt. 18:18

But to you who are listening I say: Love your enemies, do
good to those who hate you, bless those who curse you,
pray for those who mistreat you. Luke 6:27-28

For God has not given us a spirit of fear, but of power
and of love and of a sound mind.   2 Tim. 1:7 (NKJV)

But the cowardly, unbelieving, abominable, murderers,
sexually immoral, sorcerers, idolaters, and all liars
shall have their part in the lake which burns
with fire and brimstone, which is the
second death." Revelation 21:8

There are areas in our lives that can open up doors for the enemy to enter. Our decisions are powerful, and we can decide to open doors to the devil or shut them. It is our decision. The Lord has tools to help us to make good decisions. These include the Word of God, His Holy Spirit, grace and the name of Jesus. Only we can open and shut the doors. We can make the decisions, but we cannot avoid the consequences that come with those decisions. Doors that give entrance to the enemy include:

- Hatred and bitterness, including holding grudges and being critical, judgmental or jealous

- Fear, including worry, anxiety, loneliness, and looking for ways to escape or control

- Sexual sin, including pornography, fornication, homosexuality, and rape

- The occult, including witchcraft, ouiji boards, fortune telling, horoscopes, and satanism

If one or more of these doors are open in our lives, it affects our relationship with God. We can feel like He is mad at us, far away, cold or indifferent. We have difficulty reading the Bible, listening to His voice or enjoying His presence. Or, perhaps, you feel guilty all the time. If any of these things are happening to you, you probably need to shut a door to the enemy.

Testimony

*Maria was abused at a young age and never had told a soul. She held on to the bitterness her whole life until one day, when attending a school of leadership, God spoke to her.

"Talk to someone about what happened to you," He

whispered. "You have to get rid of this bitterness in your heart." Although it was very hard, she approached a leader, and told her what happened. The leader prayed that the spiritual chains around her would be broken. God set her free and then gave Maria the power to forgive, which slammed the door shut on the enemy. Currently, she is in the process of seeing her family restored. Her walk with the Lord is peaceful but strong and free from hindrances.

*name changed

Naty O. from Cordoba, shares her story:

"When I was twelve years old **the occult grabbed my attention.** I went to church with my family and thought that since I went to church, even if I participated in occult games, I would still be fine. At age thirteen, I started channeling spirits at school. From that moment I began to experience many ugly things such as hearing voices and seeing demons to the point where my parents could no longer enter my bedroom because they felt a demonic influence blocking them. I lived like this for three years, playing with the devil. By this time I no longer believed in the power of God and no one explained to me why these ugly things were happening.

At age sixteen, I had my first encounter with the Holy Spirit. I encountered the ministry of King's Castle for the first time and understood the importance of having a relationship with Jesus. At that moment, the Holy Spirit hugged me so hard, that the process of liberation began in my life. God spoke to me and showed me that I had to renounce the occult, the games and the channeling in the name of Jesus. That is how I shut the door of my life to the occult and to the enemy.

My relationship with the Holy Spirit grew so much that at night my parents would go to my room to see what was going on and find me praying in tongues in my sleep. God won my heart and showed me that His power is greater than any demonic force. I fell in love with the Holy Spirit! Never again did I play with the occult, nor even watch horror movies. I understood that I had to keep the door closed and only open the door of my heart to the Holy Spirit!"

Questions for the group / individual

1. Do you feel bitterness or unforgiveness toward someone?

2. Do you feel like it is necessary to forgive yourself?

3. Are you offended with God for something that hasn't been right in your life?

4. Do you feel burdened down with fear?

5. Is there a sexual sin that you should renounce?

6. Were you ever involved in an occult practice?[1]

How can we shut open doors in our lives?

- Repent for making bad decisions.

- Forgive those who have caused us pain. Forgiveness is a decision, not a feeling.

- Renounce any occult practices in Jesus' name.

- Ask the Holy Spirit to fill you with His presence, love and power.

When we shut the doors to the enemy:

- We can live in freedom, joy, peace and victory over sin.

- God can speak to us every day through His Word and the Holy Spirit, and we can enjoy intimacy with Him like never before.[1]

Notes and Suggested Books:

[1]De Silva, Dawna and Teresa Liebscher. *Sozo, Saved, Healed, Delivered: A Journey into Freedom with the Father, Son, and Holy Spirit.* Shippensburg, PA: Destiny Image, 2016. pp. 146-147.

ACTIVATION #35
BE SUPERNATURAL ON SOCIAL MEDIA

Go into all the world and preach the gospel to all creation.
Mark 16:15

Then the disciples went out and preached everywhere,
and the Lord worked with them and confirmed His
word by the signs that accompanied it.
Mark 16:20

The heart of God is that no one should perish. He uses all methods of evangelism in order to encounter every type of person. Today, there are many people who are stuck to the phone, Instagram, or another program. Instead of letting satan dominate the internet with pornography, bullying and lies, why shouldn't God's children use social media to change lives, bring hope, salvation, healing and deliverance?

Testimonies

Lucas was sharing Jesus with some skeptical, atheistic high school boys who were congregated outside of their school, waiting until the last minute to go inside. The Lord gave him the impression that one of them was suffering because of his parents separating, and another had back and knee pain. No one wanted to admit to either situation, so Lucas invited them to connect with him via Instagram so that they could talk to him privately if they wished. Then they disappeared into the school.

Soon after, he received an ugly message from one of the boys accusing Lucas of using Jesus to get more followers in Instagram. Lucas replied that no one had to follow him if they didn't want to, and they could use Whats App or Messenger if preferred. Just then, another message came through from the boy who suffered from knee and back pain, asking for prayer. Lucas prayed for him, over Instagram, and right afterward the boy texted back that he was completely pain free! A few minutes later the angry kid texted, "I'm so sorry. My friend was completely healed a few minutes ago after receiving your text. I'm ashamed of how I accused you. Now you are my Instagram hero!"

Lucas shared with Nathaniel about the healing over Instagram. That night, a friend from Bible college texted Nate about back pain he was experiencing. Nate remembered what Lucas had shared with him and prayed for his friend over Instagram. Immediately, all pain left! Just then, Nate received another text from a roommate of the young man who was just healed asking Nate to pray for him to be healed of pain in his body as well. So Nate prayed again, sent the message and the roommate felt all his pain leave too, and he sent Nate a text praising God for his healing!

Adrián, age 18, tells us:

"I was talking to a friend from high school on the phone,

and he told me that while cutting with a grinder, a shard of metal hit him in the eye. His retina was damaged, and it had been bothering him terribly for days. This particular friend believes in God but would always make fun of me when I'd go to church, so I never was very motivated to talk to him about Jesus. But that day I had the perfect reason to pray for him. I told him to put his hand over his eye, and then I prayed for his eye to be healed. Although nothing happened at that moment, he thanked me for praying for him that way. I was shocked! We need to always be ready to minister because you never know when God will open up an opportunity for us."

Activation:

1. Pray for your friends over social media.

2. If you know someone who is sick right now, pray for him or her. Then, send a message telling that that you are praying for his or her healing.

3. Post on your Facebook wall or on Instagram a word of knowledge or encouragement.

Example: I believe that someone has a really bad pain in the left ankle. Send me a message, and I'll pray for you to be healed.

4. Send an encouraging message to someone however the Lord directs.

Activation #36
Changing our neighborhoods

*I will give you every place where you set your foot, as I
promised Moses.* Joshua 1:3

*Let your light shine before others, that they may see your
good deeds and glorify your Father in heaven.*
Matthew 5:16

The central offices of King's Castle Argentina is located
in a needy zone in one of the suburbs of Buenos Aires.
Almost all of the staff members of the national team had
been robbed, some multiple times, when Kim and Shari
became the national directors in 2007. When Matías
arrived to serve on the staff, he was robbed twice in nine
days. The first time, he was hit on the head with a pipe
and had to go to the emergency room to get two stitches!

Shari cried out to the Lord, desperate and frustrated, praying,
"Lord! Why is this happening? Why did you give us a place in
such a dangerous area? Do we have to move?"

The voice of the Lord was clear, "Stop complaining. Get up and
take authority over the evil spirits. Use the authority I have

given you!"

So the team began to walk the streets, praying, and binding up spirits of violence, robbery, abuse and fear. The team invited the kingdom of God to come into the neighborhood (Matt. 6:10) bringing salvation, protection, peace, and joy. They prayed in tongues as well, which allowed the Holy Spirit to pray as He wished for the area. The atmosphere began to change, and the staff quit being robbed. However, they found if they let too much time go by without the prayer walks, problems would start coming back, pushing the team to get back out on the streets and pray some more.

Now, along with the EFX students, prayer walks are happening every week. The students are also working in the neighborhood and government housing development two blocks away. Recently, at one ministry gathering, there were more than eighty kids and teenagers hearing the good news of Jesus Christ!

Testimonies

As Castle staff and EFX students, **we have started going into our neighborhood to pray for the safety and protection** of our residents and businesses. We have formed groups and taken responsibility for sections to visit weekly, so we can establish relationships and follow up on conversations from previous weeks. As we share the purpose of our prayers--to make this neighborhood the safest in the city, people have begun to open up and receive prayer for more personal issues.

When Karen's group entered a neighborhood store, they told the employee what they were doing and proceeded to ask if she had any needs that they could remember in prayer. The woman, Joanna, cautiously told Karen that she had been experiencing panic attacks because of stress, due to money problems. She related that her two children were doing well, though, because some people were coming into her neighborhood each week to teach them. Her children would come home with notebooks and Bible verses to memorize and even tell her the things they had learned about God. She was thrilled that her kids were no longer causing trouble. When asked where she lived, Joanna told them that she lived in the nearby government housing, Santa Rita. With a big smile, Karen explained that her group was part of those who ministered to the kids every week.

Once Joanna learned who they were, she asked them to pray for her. Before leaving, Karen asked if they could visit Joanna at her home in the barrio, and she happily invited them to come. This was so encouraging because they had been praying for God to open homes in that area for adult small groups, and it appears that Joanna was the first answer to that prayer.

Let's take back our neighborhoods, whether it be in Buenos Aires or in your city.

Activation:

1. Walk around your neighborhood, praying for those who live in each house. Pray in the Spirit, too. Ask the Lord to give you His love for your neighborhood.

2. Enter the businesses and share with the employees that you are praying for security, protection and the blessing of God over them and their businesses. Ask them if there is something specific that you can pray for them. If they say no, smile and continue on to the next place. If they do give you a prayer request, if there isn't anyone else waiting in line, ask if you can pray for them right then. If they say no, just tell them you will pray for them later. The next time you go there, ask them if there has been a change in the situation.

3. There are many sects nowadays that are trying to convert your neighbors. But no one likes to feel like they are just another number, someone's project, nor pushed to do something. Make friends. Be nice and caring. Don't be discouraged if you are rejected the first time you offer to pray for someone. If you can assure them that you don't want anything from them, but just want to bless them in any way that you can, the day will come when they will value your friendship and prayers.

4. Memorize the names of the people in your neighborhood. Greet them by name:

"Good morning, Mr. Smith."

"Hello, Mrs. Jones, how are you today?"

"Hi Emma, everything okay?"

Everyone feels valued when you remember their names.

ACTIVATION #37
CHANGING YOUR MOOD

Rejoice always. 1 Thes. 5:16

In everything give thanks; for this is the will of God in Christ Jesus for you. 1 Thes 5:18 (NKJV)

The joy of the LORD is your strength.
Nehemiah 8:10b

You can be in a good mood every day. How? By choosing what thoughts you are going to think. Our feelings flow out of our thoughts. If you wake up, believing that you are a victim and that only bad things happen in your life, you will be in a bad mood and that will affect everyone around you. The Bible never tells us to do something without giving us the power to do it. The scripture says, "rejoice always", and the Word of God gives us the way to accomplish that command.

We are instructed to *"take every thought captive to make it obedient to Christ"* (2 Cor. 10:5). This means that we can change our thoughts! Begin to think, *'what a beautiful day. I live under the favor of God. He's watching out for me. Good things happen in my life. I'm not a victim, I am powerful!'* Begin to thank God for every blessing in your life. (Do you have food, clothes, someone who loves you, a supernatural God?) When we give thanks our attitude and environment changes, too.

You have a choice. Are you going to choose thoughts that come from the enemy to contaminate your mind or will you choose positive thoughts from God that bring joy, favor and gives the Holy Spirit opportunity to bless you? If you have to cut off friendships that drag you down, get off of social media, change your cell phone number, giving it to just those who will help you make good choices, it is worth the effort. You are a powerful person who makes powerful choices—and the choice you make today will lay the foundation for your future. God will reward you and give you His peace and joy as everyday you *give thanks; for this is the will of God in Christ Jesus concerning you.*

Testimony

When we opened the ministry of King's Castle in Southern Argentina, we traveled as a team to the Patagonia. We had borrowed a vehicle in which the seven staff members could fit legally—although it was tight. It was a very hot day and as the temperature climbed the air conditioner grew weaker until it was like traveling in an oven. The team members told us about a game that they used to play where if someone said something negative, they would lose. So, if without thinking someone remarked, "I am so hot," they would have to quickly remedy the remark with a positive ending like "...it must be that God is getting me ready to be a missionary in Saudi Arabia." So throughout the rest of the trip we heard comments such as:

"I am so sweaty...but what a great way to lose weight."

"I am so tired of sitting... but thank God that we don't have to stand all the way to the Patagonia!"

"This trip is so long... but so thankful that we aren't traveling by horse!"

"My hair is full of dust... but I like the 'hair plastered to my head' look."

How we laughed at all of the creative commentaries! And while it was still uncomfortable, these choices changed the atmosphere from frustration to joy.

Activation:

1. Write down thoughts that you have when you are in a "bad mood".

2. For each one of those thoughts, write a positive thought to replace it.

Examples: I'm ugly / I'm a creative work of God, unique and beautiful.

Everyone treats me badly. / I am not a victim, I am powerful because a powerful God lives inside of me.

No one loves me. / God (and my mom, grandmother, friend, you fill in the blank...) loves me.

I can't do anything right. / The truth is, I am good at _____.

3. Write a list of blessings that you have in your life. It can include people, activities you enjoy, vacations you took, belongings, pets....

4. Give thanks for every thing on your list.

5. Ask the Lord to help you to see your life with His eyes. (because He sees your potential) and that He would help you to cultivate a happy and thankful heart.

ACTIVATION #38
DECLARATIONS WILL CHANGE YOUR LIFE

Death and life are in the power of the tongue, and those who love it will eat its fruit. Prov. 18:21 (NKJV)

I will not die but live, and will proclaim what the LORD has done. Psalm 118:17

When the Lord created the earth He declared each aspect into existence. "Let there be light," and the light began to shine, even though the sun had not yet been created. The spiritual world is the same. Instead of declaring things that have their roots in the kingdom of darkness, such as I'm useless, I'm stupid, I'm ugly, or I can't, let's use our words to declare life and encouragement. I **can** do all things though Christ, I have the mind of Jesus, I am important in God's kingdom, I'm learning, and I never give up are some examples of words of life. Let's declare words of life over ourselves and others.

Testimony

Shari remembers:

"We pastored in a little town of about 1800 people in

the Upper Peninsula of Michigan, where the bears and wolves outnumbered the humans. I read a book that talked about the prayer of Jabez, based on *1 Chronicles 4:10,* and was impacted by its message. From that day until our children left our home, each morning, in our family devotions, we would finish our Bible reading and prayer with everyone reciting this prayer:

> *Oh that you would bless me indeed and enlarge my territory, that Your hand would be upon me, and that You would keep me from evil, that I would cause no pain.*

Two years later, the Lord took us to Argentina, to work with new church plants and build churches for the indigenous people, the Wichi. Soon after, we were given the privilege and responsibility of working with the ministry of Castillo del Rey Argentina and our influence was extended to include youth around the nation, and this influence touched other nations as well. Our children also have been given much influence in the kingdom of God. Your words have power, and what you declare in prayer sets things into motion because you are following God's example."

Activation:

1. Write down ten declarations to speak over yourself. For example: I am a powerful child of God, I hear God's voice all the time, I'm honest, I have the mind of Christ.

2. Write down ten declarations to speak over your family. For example: The love of God flows in my family, we respect one another, my family is prospering, my father goes to

church, my mom is strong and healthy.

3. Declare these truths every day until they come to pass. Write down the dates that you see the changes happen and thank God for every one.

Group Activation:

Ask everyone to think of something to declare over your team, ministry, or community. Everyone takes a turn proclaiming their declaration while everyone else responds, "Amen!" or another word/phrase of affirmation.

Examples:
I declare that this team is guided by the Holy Spirit and full of His Presence! (Amen!)

I declare that each family represented will follow Jesus! (Yes, Lord!)

I declare that we will see miracles when we share about Jesus! (Amen!)

Suggested Books,

Victorious Mindsets by Steve Backlund
Any other books by Steve and Wendy Backlund

ACTIVATION #39
DREAMING WITH GOD

How precious to me are your thoughts, God! How vast is
the sum of them! Were I to count them, they would
outnumber the grains of sand—when I awake,
I am still with you. Psalm 139:17-18

For we are God's handiwork, created in Christ Jesus to
do good works, which God prepared in advance for
us to do. Ephesians. 2:10

"For I know the plans I have for you," declares the LORD,
"plans to prosper you and not to harm you, plans
to give you hope and a future". Jeremiah 29:11

You are not a mistake. God made you with love and for a purpose. He began to dream about you before you were conceived. He has many dreams to plant into your heart. Plus, there are gifts and talents that are hidden inside you, which He wants you to develop through the help of the Holy Spirit. It is also important to understand your role in the process. You have to put forth effort in order to excel in anything, through study, practice, sacrifice and hard work. But isn't it worth it, to work together with God in order to fulfill your destiny?

Testimonies

One day, Kim, challenged our national CDR team to write a list of dreams and goals that each member wanted to complete in five years. Zeba wrote down his dreams, as well as his goals for his spiritual life, career, family, and education. Two years later, he approached Kim to show that although the five years had not yet passed by, many of the goals and dreams on his paper had already come to pass! God is faithful to work with us to complete our dreams.

Juan Torres, at age fifteen, received a missionary call to France. His calling turned into a dream to minister in that country. Years later, he became engaged to Naty O., who also shared His calling. After completing Bible school, they got married and began to work faithfully in their church as youth leaders, while Juan worked toward a teaching degree. Although it seemed like the dream was beyond their reach, they continued working faithfully with their teens, as well as in their secular jobs. At one point, it seemed like nothing was happening concerning their call to France, and they began to wonder if they were only to pray for France instead of going there as missionaries.

Nevertheless, seeing the faithfulness of Juan and Naty, fifteen years after receiving the call, God opened doors for Juan to travel to France and meet with church leaders there. Every time he ministered, the Lord backed up his sermon with healings and miracles. The French pastors invited Juan's family to come and work in France as missionaries and help them minister to the youth of their nation. Juan, Naty and son, Martin, are preparing to go even now.

What are your dreams? What is God dreaming about your life?

Activation: Dreaming with God

1. Spend time dreaming with God about what you would do if you knew you couldn't fail.

2. What would you attempt to do for the kingdom of God if you had no fear?

3. What would you do if money was no option?

4. Ask God to plant His dreams in your heart. He probably has already done so.

5. Make a list of thirty dreams that you would like to fulfill if you had no fear, if there was no possibility of failure and if money was no object. Your dream list can include spiritual goals, places to visit, your future family, career or any area where you can dream dreams.

Activation #40 — Seeking Wisdom

The fear of the LORD is the beginning of wisdom: and the knowledge of the holy is understanding. Prov. 9:10

If any of you lacks wisdom, you should ask God, who gives generously to all without finding fault, and it will be given to you. James 1:5

For wisdom is more precious than rubies, and nothing you desire can compare with her. Prov. 8:11

The Bible tells us that wisdom is based in God. It also tells us that those who do not recognize that there is a God are foolish. One can spend years earning degrees, but the same person, even though he has gained much knowledge, can make decisions that will damage his career, family or health. When we read the Bible and spend time with God, He imparts His wisdom to help us be successful in life. Proverbs assures us that wisdom provides many benefits, such as health, strength, protection, provision, honor, riches, authority, and the favor of God. Wisdom brings blessings over every part of our life.

Testimonies

Noelia tells us:

"I was asking the Lord to give me wisdom, but it came in a way I wasn't expecting.

One day I was alone, painting one of many doors that I had to paint, and very angry because the people who had committed to come and help hadn't come through on their promises. I was tired, arguing with God about how things never went as quickly as I wished, how long He was taking in fulfilling my calling, how people didn't come through on projects, and God interrupted me.

'I allow my dreams to *gestate* inside of you, but they are mine and subject to my times. If you want something to be born in your time, you will probably cause a spiritual abortion. Let my dreams gestate until the time I say they should come to pass.'"

Lucas M. shares:

"I was at home and I realized that I had five boxes of milk that had reached the expiration date. Time had passed quickly, and I hadn't been drinking as much as usual. I went outside to throw the milk away, and just then I felt in my heart not to do so. These boxes of milk might be a blessing to someone.

I began to walk down my street and asked God who I was supposed to give them to since some people would be offended to be offered milk with an expiration date on the same day. Three blocks later, the Lord highlighted a particular house, so I went up and knocked on the door. A lady looked out the window, and I explained that I had milk to give away. Surprised, she hurried to the door and opened it. I gave her the milk and turned to go when she said to me, 'May God bless you richly!'

'Do you believe in God?' I asked.

'Yes, I'm a Christian,' she answered, 'and with this milk I know that God is thinking about me. I have three kids and it's been several days since I have been able to buy milk.'

I still had two more boxes to give away. I walked two more blocks and saw a grandma walking down the street. I approached her and explained that I had two boxes of milk to give away that would need to be used in the next day or so. She was thrilled to get them.

'God will recompense you for this,' she told me. She also was a believer!

How great is God, to use five boxes of milk to bless two families and remind them that He is taking care of them."

Activation:

1. Read Prov. Chapters 3, 4 and 8. Find references to wisdom.

2. Make a list of the benefits that wisdom brings. Determine to be someone who seeks wisdom.

3. Ask God which areas of your life need more wisdom.

4. Make a list of five important decisions that you need to make in the next month. Ask God to give you wisdom to do the right thing for each.

5. Reach a chapter of Proverbs each day that corresponds with the date. For example, the first day of the month, read Proverbs 1. On the fifth day of the month read chapter 5, and so on.

WHEN IT SEEMS
LIKE NOTHING HAPPENED

We walk by faith, not by sight.   2 Cor. 5:7

At times our prayers don't bring the answers that we want at the moment, and we can become frustrated. Each person is unique, and the Lord loves and deals with each one distinctly. Our part is to pray as the Bible teaches us, obey the Holy Spirit and leave the results in God's hands.

If we do not see a healing happen instantly, we cannot blame the other person for not having sufficient faith. The dead man that Jesus raised didn't have a drop of faith in him. We shouldn't blame ourselves either. In the same way that we shouldn't touch the glory that comes when someone gets healed, neither should we be weighed down with guilt when we pray and do not see results especially since sometimes the results come in the next day or two. Nevertheless, we can ask God for more understanding, more love and more of His power later when we get alone with Him.

Afterward, we try again, knowing that Jesus instructed us to ask Father God "that His kingdom would come," and that kingdom includes health, peace, joy, freedom, provision, and more. Our motto should be: "we are still learning" and we understand that we have to practice in order to learn.

Nobody can preach perfectly without having learned some principles and spent time practicing. One cannot play an instrument, cook a tasty meal or build something impressive without learning and practicing first. The gifts of the Spirit are given by the Holy Spirit, but we need instruction and practice to understand how to use them with love, humility and power. They are weapons we can use against spiritual strongholds and demonic mentalities. One word of knowledge can disarm years of the enemy's lies. One prayer of faith can free someone who is bound by demons and one healing can give someone the understanding of his/her value in the eyes of God.

Testimonies

Melissa, (age 18) one of the girls on our national team, left for her first treasure hunt. Returning with her group, she announced, "I failed nine times!" Every person that she had approached either wasn't interested in what she had to say, wasn't the one on her list or just flat out told her to get lost.

Two weeks later, Melissa was in charge of a training weekend in the province of Misiones. One of the girls attending was a fourteen year old who couldn't straighten her legs all the way and walked with her knees in a slightly bent position, which kept her from running or dancing choreographies with the rest of the group. When Melissa saw Blanca walking carefully to her seat, she felt compassion rise up inside of her and asked the group,

"Do you all think that Jesus wants Blanca to walk this way her whole life?"

The group agreed that, no, they didn't think that was Jesus' desire for Blanca. So Melissa called the group to surround the girl and pray for God to lengthen the ligaments and tendons so that she could stand up straight. The kids began to pray, believing that God's will was to heal Blanca, and they watched as the tendons grew and she stood straight for the first time in her entire life! She jumped and ran and danced the entire weekend!

Thank God that Melissa hadn't believed the lie that the supernatural wasn't part of her inheritance or Blanca may never have experienced her miracle that day!

Testimony of frustration

Lucas M. from the Province of Mendoza begins:

"We were two fourteen-year-olds with a hunger for God and the supernatural. We were passionate to see miracles. One day we were at a church service where we were praying for miracles and Darío, my friend, had a broken wrist. A cast covered the lower part of his arm and hand. We had so much faith and I said, 'Darío, lets go outside and take off your cast. I believe that you are healed.'

We went behind the church, found a faucet, put his cast under the flow of water, and using the water and a knife that we'd found in the kitchen, began to cut the soggy cast off his wrist. A few minutes later, his wrist was free.

But Darío said to me, 'Lucas, my wrist really hurts. Actually my whole hand really hurts!'

So we prayed even harder, with lots of faith. Nevertheless, he repeated, 'My hand really hurts!' His hand began to swell and his mother was mad at us for taking the cast off without any permission or x-rays to show he was healed.

I was super frustrated with God. For months I refused to pray for any healing or miracle. In my heart I was saying, 'You left me alone when you could have performed a miracle. Now I don't trust you anymore to help me if I try it again.'"

* * * * * * *

What will you do when it appears that you failed? Or when it looks like God didn't answer your prayers. Are you going to decide that you can't live a supernatural life with your Supernatural Dad, or are you going to keep on going until you see the power of God manifested in your life?

* * * * * * *

Six months later... Lucas continues his story:

"We were at a prayer meeting, Darío, another friend and myself. A man from the church approached us at the end of the service and asked us if we would go to the hospital and pray for two kids with cancer. It was about 10:00 PM. He insisted and gave us the hospital room numbers, so we went to the hospital with him. Both kids were about eight years old, and both only had a couple of days to live. Visiting hours had been over long before, so we had to get creative with how to get inside. We used our other friend to distract the guard while we crawled under the security counter and ran silently through the halls. As we were doing this, we kept thinking, this is so crazy! The last time we took a risk it didn't turn out so good!

We arrived at the first room. The scene was somber. The mother who sat beside her son as he was slowly dying had no faith. The boy's arms were skeletal, and his head was bald from all the chemotherapy treatments. Darío and I looked at each other. We felt no faith but we prayed over the boy for healing, anyway, and then left.

Entering the next room, the scene was similar. We prayed again and didn't feel anything.

We thanked the mom for letting us pray and then left.

A week later, there were two women waiting at the door of the church when we arrived.

'Aren't you the boys who came to pray for our kids last week?' one of them asked.

'Uh, yeah,' we admitted, hesitantly.

'Since the moment you boys prayed, our kids started getting better. Not only did they not die in the three days allotted them, but in the last scans, not one cancer cell could be found in their bodies!' said one of the mothers.

One month later, both boys were discharged, completely well. We could hardly believe it! Thank God that we didn't decide to give up praying for miracle, even though we had failed so miserably. From that day until this (10 years later), I haven't stopped seeing miracles."

Authors' note: Lucas and Darío are much wiser now and would never cut off a cast without having an x-ray taken first. A doctor should affirm whatever miracle that God did and corroborate it with medical tests. It isn't a lack of faith to act wisely. Plus, the medical records prove that the miracle happened.

Not taking medicine won't heal you. The power of God is what heals, and he can heal us while we are taking medicine and completing treatments. Therefore, when you pray for someone's healing and the person feels a difference, encourage the person to go back to the doctor and get it checked out. It will be a wonderful testimony for the medical community, and the doctor can change the medication or treatment accordingly.

The truth is that if Jesus is your savior, you are part of a supernatural family. Your Dad has lots of resources in the universe and is willing to give you the Holy Spirit, His gifts and power to help you complete your purpose on the earth. Father God has dreams and adventures for you every day, and if you learn to hear Him and decide to obey Him, you will have a part of bringing His Kingdom upon the earth, (Matt. 10:7-8).

A Note from Kim

Shari and I are passionate about what God is doing on the earth with this generation. In the midst of volcanoes exploding, earthquakes trembling and wars breaking out for the hearts and minds of the societies on the planet, we can see beyond all of these things. God has placed a vision in our hearts to see this generation ignited with a holy love and passion for Jesus.

When all else seems to be weakening under the stress and strain of moral implosion, the church has been chosen to call down the fire of heaven, not the fire of destruction, but the fire that has built the church since the day of Pentecost. This Holy Spirit fire is more than an emotion and more than an impulse. This fire is the same fire that brings us to the feet of Jesus in repentance, the same that fills us up with the power of heaven and the same that sends us to the nations to make disciples.

We pray as you read this book that a hunger will burst forth in your life for the supernatural power of Jesus. One of our favorite expressions in working with this generation is that we are working in a laboratory. Don't be afraid to take risks. As Jesus said, the Holy Spirit is our teacher.

I hope you had fun reading this book and may it produce in

you a lifetime of adventures with Jesus. May His Kingdom come and His will be done on the earth as it is in heaven.

By the way, my name is on this book as a co-author with my bride of 36 years, but except for this note, she did all the writing. However, we have lived these stories together and want to see so much more!

We have to raise our own financial support to continue working with the youth of Argentina and Latin America. If you are interested in helping us and King's Castle Argentina financially, you can do so at: http://s1.ag.org/ksbab

Sincerely,
Kim Babcock